THE GRADUATE STUDY OF EDUCATION

THE GRADUATE STUDY OF EDUCATION

Report of the Harvard Committee

HARVARD UNIVERSITY PRESS

Cambridge, Massachusetts · 1966

FOREWORD

A curious quality of education is that, while most persons experience it intimately, few study it in any serious way at all. In our hurry to purvey or consume it, we pause infrequently to question what we are up to. We are alternately too brash and too reactionary and always, it seems, too busy to decide which and why. More importantly, we are too caught up with pressing numbers and immediate crises to decide what we should be doing in the first place. So we stumble on, giving and receiving schooling without full reflection on the truly sophisticated and ethical practice it involves.

Presumably it is one function of universities to illumine the purposes and practices of the institutions of society, schools among them. Schools of education would seem to bear this responsibility, but casual inspection finds most of them not only overwhelmed with the magnitude of merely keeping the schools staffed, but also confused over how, even if there were time, resources, and imagination, to organize themselves to study the enterprise which they service. Further inquiry shows that schools of education differ widely in size, tradition, setting, and stated purpose. Clearly no single answer will solve for all of them the dual problem of responsibility for great numbers of students and confusion of purpose. Each institution or group of similar institutions must find its own solutions to these and other problems.

It was with these concerns that the Committee on the Graduate Study of Education was appointed at Harvard in 1964. The committee was charged to ask how this faculty of education, with its own set of strengths and weaknesses, could best use its resources to study and improve the quality of education. It was asked to set priorities and provide a focus that would make sense for this particular university at this particular time. The faculty actions that followed (which, it should be noted, did not necessarily conform to the suggestions of the committee) are now made available to the community at large, as perhaps a useful example of how one school of education has assessed its function. The report does not recommend a particular detailed national blueprint; quite the contrary. It does suggest, however, an approach to the analysis of the problem faced by the committee. It speaks to Harvard and presumes little more. Yet it does speak, if with restraint, to the general question of how the study of education might be construed anywhere.

James Perkins, in his recent essays on American universities, *Universities in Transition* (Princeton, 1966), has rightly argued for a constructive balance between the three major functions of the academic community: inquiry, teaching, and service. Almost since their inception, however, schools of education have been out of sensible balance. Swamped with students (and pressed with an understandable legislative demand to supply the schools) they have had to put disproportionate energy into teaching. Pressed since the early part of this century to assist in setting up a school system that was growing at a prodigious rate, "service" in the form of short-run surveys, "workshops," and the rest were also exaggerated. What lagged was inquiry, and it is the inadequacy of research and development in education that has received much recent notice. Perkins argues that a true university must not only provide in the three areas he mentions but also so organize itself that its research enriches its teaching and service and that the latter elements give the former relevance and rigor. The imbalance in schools of education begs for correction, and it is to this problem that the present report speaks with considerable force.

The other serious difficulty faced by the community of professionals in education is the inadequacy of resources, both human and financial. It is not that there are not enough persons in the field; indeed there are more degrees of every description granted in this country in education than in any other. It is rather that there are not enough absolutely first-rate people, either academically or in terms of commitment, to move the field forward. Sadly, education classes in most universities are drawn from a low academic level of the student body, and from the best of this group (and from most of its males irrespective of quality) educational leadership is drawn. There are exceptions, of course; but the evidence of weak professional leadership and shoddy scholarship makes the general conclusion irrefutable. Service in the schools is low-status work; but it should not be. Scholarship on the problems of schooling is neglected, but it ought not to be. Somehow, greater numbers of bright and committed people must be attracted to and held in this enterprise and the study illuminating the craft of teaching and counseling raised up. No one institution can take on these tasks alone. The Harvard committee's recommendation for concentration on scholarship and on advanced training is a recognition both of these as but parts of the large problem and of this university's particular traditions and strengths.

Money is also a difficulty, but one easier to correct than inadequate leadership. As schools of education have had large numbers of students, particularly evening and extension students, they have become in many universities (not including Harvard, it should be stressed) major sources of income for the institution as a whole. All too rarely, however, has this income gone into support of teacher education; more often it has been diverted elsewhere. As a result, the low per capita cost of schools of education quietly appeals as much to some administrators as it appears (ironically) as the butt of ridicule of other more prestigious and financially better-favored departments of the university. Educating teachers is a serious, costly business. To do it right one needs strong libraries and film collections, varied faculty including master teachers and counselors in schools, and a wide range of school materials that prospective teachers can assess and learn to use. No school of education in the United States comes anywhere close to having the financial resources to do the teaching (or, for that matter, the research) job right. This fact cannot be avoided.

In many respects the Harvard report can be called remarkably conservative. It does not offer a new conception of "education": it deliberately disavows "education" as some kind of science or discipline. It suggests no radical pattern of organization or areas to be approached. It is an argument for balance and improvement of the best we know now. It is, thus, more a blueprint for reaching adequately our present goals than a statement of new direction. Given the popularity of educational "innovation" in these days, this conservative nature of the report may indeed *be* radical!

Appendix B outlines the details of faculty action on the report. Most important was the endorsement of an increased emphasis on doctoral studies and scholarship. While, owing to inadequate time, the committee did not specify the details of doctoral work to the extent of those for the master's degree, faculty committees have made progress on these matters during the 1965-66 academic year, as described in Appendix C. A much strengthened "clinical" master's degree has been approved, though in a more flexible form than the committee recommended. Key to this is an emphasis on a well-supervised, paid internship of up to a year's duration. Studies at Harvard would be of one year's length. Postdoctoral programs (or, more appropriately, "midcareer" sabbatical programs) and short-term nondegree institutes focused on currently critical areas have been endorsed.

The committee's rejection of a "discipline" of education is best symbolized by the adoption of six "areas" of faculty organization: teaching, guidance, administration, humanities, social sciences, and psychology. The first three focus on "clinical" problems: the teaching of the various subjects (the natural sciences, languages, and so forth), counseling, administration. The latter three include faculty from the traditional disciplines who are working through these to illumine and find solutions for problems in education. The areas overlap, and faculty have assumed membership in two or more; they differ from traditional "departments" in this sense and in the sense that the areas do not have budgetary responsibilities. Further, the areas symbolize the faculty's commitment both to applied and theoretical fields, to a carefully contrived wedding of theory and practice both in inquiry into the nature of the enterprise and in the training of practitioners. They imply a plan to maintain both the perspective of aloofness and the leavening of involvement, the wisdom gained both from detachment and commitment. The search for this mix is nothing new, but no institution has so far achieved it. The committee attempted to find an approach for this particular community, but the power of its argument should provoke useful consideration elsewhere.

The following report is, really, an affirmation that university schools of education can make a significant difference not only in supplying the raw material for the nation's schools but also the significant ideas upon which education must rest. It rests now with the faculty to see that this optimism was not misplaced.

In order to give the reader a sense of the Harvard context of this report, a historical sketch of the study of education at Harvard appears as Appendix A. That sketch, by Arthur Powell, reminds one of the difficulties universities have in changing and of the dangerous ease with which they can plod on with undefined goals and largely irrelevant activities. Appendix D gives a graphic and tabular statistical view of the Harvard Graduate School of Education over the past two and a half decades.

The thanks of the faculty are due to the committee and particularly to its wise and patient chairman. The staff which labored for it—Peter Carbone, Michael Katz, and Jane B. Conant—deserves high praise. We are grateful for the patience and time given by countless colleagues at Harvard and elsewhere. The scope of the study would not have been possible without the generosity of the Carnegie Corporation, and particularly the interest and encouragement of its now acting president, Alan Pifer.

Theodore R. Sizer
Dean, Harvard Graduate School
of Education

Cambridge, Massachusetts
May 1966

ACKNOWLEDGMENTS

The committee gratefully acknowledges its indebtedness to the many colleagues, both within and outside the University, who contributed in a number of ways to the preparation of this report. Institutional affiliations are those given at the time the report was first issued.

Persons who met with the committee or its staff included Hugo E. Beck, University of Chicago; George Z. F. Bereday, Teachers College, Columbia; James H. Blessing, U.S. Office of Education, Washington, D.C.; Merle L. Borrowman, University of Wisconsin; Norman J. Boyan, Stanford; Donald R. Brown, Harvard; Robert N. Bush, Stanford; Daniel H. Calhoun, Harvard; Roald F. Campbell, University of Chicago; James B. Conant, President, Emeritus, Harvard; Dana M. Cotton, Harvard; Abner Crabb, George Peabody College for Teachers; Lawrence A. Cremin, Teachers College, Columbia; Thomas E. Crooks, Harvard; Glenn Eye, University of Wisconsin; Alan D. Ferguson, U.S. Office of Education, Washington, D.C.; John Guy Fowlkes, University of Wisconsin; G. Ernst Giesecke, University of Chicago; Neal Gross, Harvard; Paul R. Hanna, Stanford; John Hosler, University of Wisconsin; Cyril O. Houle, University of Chicago; Chris D. Kehas, University of Chicago; Leopold E. Klopfer, University of Chicago; Myron Lieberman, Rhode Island College; George F. F. Lombard, Harvard; Robert L. McCaul, Jr., University of Chicago; Raymond C. Norris, George Peabody College for Teachers; Frederick A. Olafson, Harvard; I. James Quillen, Stanford; Herman G. Richey, University of Chicago; Felix C. Robb, George Peabody College for Teachers; Phillip J. Rulon, Harvard; Jonas Soltis, Teachers

College, Columbia; Julian C. Stanley, Jr., University of Wisconsin; Wilson Thiede, University of Wisconsin; Harold Weisberg, Brandeis; Joseph Young, Harvard.

Those who corresponded with the committee about various aspects of the study included Glenn C. Atkyns, University of Connecticut; C. E. Beeby, Harvard; Robert L. Belenky, Harvard; Henry S. Bissex, Harvard; Arthur S. Bolster, Harvard; Richard G. Brown, Phillips Exeter Academy, Exeter, New Hampshire; Carl Cohen, Harvard; Adam Curle, Harvard; Russell G. Davis, Harvard; Mary S. Engel, Harvard; A. Irving Forbes, Harvard; William D. Frankena, University of Michigan; James H. Grew, Phillips Academy, Andover, Massachusetts; Robert E. Herriott, Florida State University; Harold L. Hodgkinson, Bard College; A. John Holden, Jr., Commissioner of Education, State of Vermont; James G. Holland, Harvard; Christopher Jencks, Institute for Policy Studies, Washington, D.C.; Kenneth J. Jones, Jr., Harvard; Michael M. Kalagian, J. Sterling Morton High Schools and Junior College, Cicero, Illinois; Douglas T. Kenny, Harvard; Owen B. Kiernan, Commissioner of Education, Commonwealth of Massachusetts; Edward Landy, Harvard; Eugene C. Lee, Emory University; Gerald S. Lesser, Harvard; Robert D. Lewis, Lexington Public Schools, Lexington, Massachusetts; Paul Marsh, Massachusetts Education Study, Boston, Massachusetts; Esther E. Matthews, Harvard; Philip E. McPherson, Pittsburgh Public Schools, Pittsburgh, Pennsylvania; Peter F. Neumeyer, Harvard; Helen M. Popp, Harvard; Arthur G. Powell, Harvard; Don K. Price, Harvard; Anne Roe, Harvard; Rose E. Sabaroff, Harvard; Edleff H. Schwaab, Harvard; Albert O. Smith, Milton Academy, Milton, Massachusetts; Robert Ulich, James Bryant Conant Professor of Education, Emeritus, Harvard; Fletcher G. Watson, Harvard; Sheldon G. Weeks, Harvard; Joel S. Weinberg, Simmons College; Judith B. Wentz, Educational Research Council of Greater Cleveland, Cleveland, Ohio; David V. Widder, Harvard.

The committee is grateful to the following persons and institutions for supplying information about their activities: Robert H. Bauernfeind, Northern Illinois University; The Brookings Institution, Washington, D.C.; Clinton I. Chase, Indiana University; T. Clinton Cobb, Michigan State University; William W. Cooley, University of Pittsburgh; Luvern L. Cunningham, University of Chicago; Paul L. Dressel, Michigan State University; Ward Edinger, State University of New York at Albany; Educational Testing Service, Princeton, New Jersey; N. A. Fattu, Indiana University; Lita Binns Fejos, Wenner-Gren Foundation for Anthropological Research, New York City; Fels Research Institute for the Study of Human Development, Antioch College; Lawrence D. Fish, University of Oregon; Bill J. Fullerton, Arizona State University; Gesell Institute of Child Development, New Haven, Connecticut; Leslie P. Greenhill, Pennsylvania State University; Egon G. Guba, Ohio State University; Armand L. Hunter, Michigan State University; Institute of Administrative Research, Teachers College, Columbia; Institute for Developmental Studies, New York Medical College; Adelaide Jablonsky, Yeshiva University; David R. Krathwohl, Michigan State University; Richard E. Lawrence, American Association of Colleges for Teacher Education, Washington, D.C.; James D. MacConnell, Stanford; William P. McLure, University of Illinois; National Council for the Social Studies, National Education Association, Washington, D.C.; National Institute of Mental Health, Washington, D.C.; Kenneth G. Nelson, U.S. Office of Education, Washington, D.C.; Henry J. Otto, University of Texas; Paul V. Petty, University of New Mexico; Earl M. Ramer, University of Tennessee at Knoxville; Arliss L. Roaden, Ohio State University; Maurice F. Seay, Michigan State University; Ozzie G. Simmons, University of Colorado; Maurice J. Thomas, University of Pittsburgh; Rickel Twersky, Research Institute for the Study of Man, New York City; University of California at Berkeley; University High School, Urbana, Illinois; Dorolese H. Wardwell, University of Minnesota; Carl E. Wedekind, University of Pittsburgh; J. Weisbrodt, Purdue University.

Thanks are due to the many Harvard graduate students and other interested persons who provided helpful comments.

The committee also wishes to express its thanks to Anne Smith, who helped to prepare the manuscript for publication, and to Blair McElroy, who edited the manuscript and prepared the index.

CONTENTS

THE GRADUATE STUDY OF EDUCATION

INTRODUCTION

In the spring of 1964, a committee of the Harvard Faculty of Education was appointed by Dean Theodore R. Sizer to consider how the graduate study of education should properly be conceived in the setting of a strong independent university, and to make recommendations regarding such study at Harvard in particular. The Committee on the Graduate Study of Education was encouraged to frame its deliberations in the broadest possible terms, to consider aims and purposes, organization and content, realities and possibilities. It was advised to free its thinking from undue preoccupation with Harvard matters by initially conceiving the issues in abstract terms as they might confront any independent American university with considerable strength in research. Yet its ultimate purpose was understood to be the formulation of proposals with specific reference to Harvard's resources and responsibilities. In the present report, we set forth the substance of our work as members of this committee.

In the course of our work, we have indeed striven to place our primary concern for the study of education at Harvard within a broader context. Through consultations with educators at other institutions and with others in a position to shed light on our problems, through studies of other universities and of Harvard's own past, through readings and discussions concerning national currents and developments in related professions, we have tried to educate ourselves as to the larger social background against which any significant proposals on education must take shape. We have not, however, attempted to produce a systematic study of this background; we offer here neither a piece of sociological research nor a specimen of historical scholarship. Nor have we attempted to write a universal blueprint for the graduate study of education, a master plan applicable to all university situations. Our primary effort has been directed rather toward the shaping of educational proposals for Harvard, which shall, however, be informed by the relevant facts and supported by pertinent general considerations.

In the presentation of our report, we therefore take as our major focus the recommendations we have to offer with respect to Harvard, introducing only as much of the background material available to us as seems necessary to explain the course of our deliberations. Such explanation we have, however, insofar as possible, attempted to provide: we have striven to expose, for the reader's independent judgment, the problems encountered, the alternatives initially considered, and the arguments ultimately found compelling. We hope that such explanatory discussion may prove to have relevance beyond the borders of the Harvard community, and independently of agreement on our final proposals. These proposals themselves may, moreover, be of wider interest, provided they are properly understood not as rigid formulas but as experimental notions motivated by stated considerations of fact and principle.

The extreme breadth of the committee's instructions constituted an initial obstacle that, in a curious way, was counterbalanced by the severe limitation of time at our disposal. Had we had more time, we might have gotten lost in a maze of unrewarding detail. With only one year at our disposal, we soon realized we had to devote ourselves primarily to general issues affecting our practice and to eschew fundamental consideration of individual program requirements or operational problems. We have thus aimed at the level of policy as it reflects a guiding conception of the graduate study of education or affects the quality or development of such study in the university. Starting from existing resources and practices as a base, we asked ourselves how the university should ideally conceive its responsibilities for the study of education in the world as it now is and as it promises to be.

This fundamental question has led us into numerous and complexly linked issues. What is the proper scope of the study of education, and how may it be structured within the university? What, in general, is the suitable role of professional study within a university setting? How are the demands of scholarship, research, professional training and service to be adjusted to one another? What principles of integration may facilitate such mutual adjustment? Is there a fundamental science of education, or a unifying set of foundational studies, or perhaps some form of common training experience or other device that may lend coherence to the various demands of educational study?

How should such study, furthermore, be oriented to the world outside the university? Should it, for example, be organized so as to follow the lead of professional practice and the existing structure of professional roles, or should it set itself the task of revising practice and restructuring roles? What, further, should be its relations to social problems arising within the sphere of professional concern? Can it calmly disregard them without threat to its integrity and keep its attention focused on abstract questions above the battle? Conversely, can it find realistic ways to express engagement in social issues without compromising either its scholarly standards or professional authority?

Aside from the scope of educational study and its relations to university, profession, and society, there are related problems that concern rather its internal organization and its execution. How, for example, should such study be divided for the purposes of instruction and research, and how may the isolating effects latent in any such division be overcome? What should degrees in education represent, and how should programs leading to such degrees be conceived? How may clinical practice, internship, and supervision be fruitfully joined with scholarly and research training? How is research itself to be developed and organized in a field where the social impact of research is relatively direct and of far-reaching significance? What sorts of professional roles should be envisaged as accessible to graduates of education programs? How may recruitment of the ablest students be improved? How should the roles of faculty members be conceived, and how may their duties be most fruitfully allocated?

This brief survey of issues will give some inkling of the tangle of deliberations underlying our proposals. It will also, by its display of complexity, underline the importance of taking these proposals in context and applying them in an experimental spirit. The scheme we have chosen for presenting our deliberations and proposals is as follows. In Part I, we deal with aims, ideals, and responsibilities. Considering the ideals of educational study inherited from the past and the current situation with regard to such study at Harvard, we explore several alternative orientations that might be adopted in the future and recommend a particular one, elaborating the reasons behind our choice. In Part II, we treat of general instrumentalities consonant with the orientation recommended, and, if not entailed by it, then at least supported by considerations in harmony with it. Here, for instance, we make recommendations regarding such matters as the organization of educational study, the major priorities that seem to us desirable, and other topics with import for all aspects of the study of education at Harvard. In Part III, we present recommendations of narrower scope that affect particular aspects or branches of educational study. There, for example, we discuss the structure of programs leading to master's and doctor's degrees, and offer recommendations concerning postdoctoral study. We also outline certain proposals regarding the conduct of research, and offer suggestions for the future development of the several areas of educational study. A concluding statement points up some of the implications of the foregoing discussions and attempts to set forth their general significance.

PART I

AIMS AND ORIENTATIONS

THE STUDY OF EDUCATION

In recent reports and public discussions of the study of education, by far the strongest emphasis has been put on the preparation of teachers. Certainly, major educational debates in the past decade have centered on the nature and control of the teacher's training and the sort of knowledge presumed most useful to the teacher in his work. The study of education has, for various reasons, become dominated by the supposed requirements of teacher preparation, and the very conception of such study has been identified in the public mind with that of an independent professional subject.

The limitations of such a conception have also, however, become increasingly evident. Cut off from its natural links with developments in pure research and scholarship, professional study tends to wither. Conversely, isolated from problems of professional practice, pure learning is diminished in relevance and power. The study of education, in particular, needs to be freed from being narrowly viewed as a separate professional subject, and given an interpretation broad enough to encompass the diverse outlooks of the researcher and scholar as well as the technologist and practitioner. The particular strength of the study of education in a university setting is that it is capable of supporting such a broad interpretation.

The Graduate School of Education at Harvard has attempted to embody such an interpretation in its own structure and operations. Heir to the mixed ideology of graduate educational study of the past, it has, in recent years especially, striven to contain its various strands, making room, under its own auspices, for multiple confrontations between research, scholarship, and practice.

The early development of university departments of education in the late nineteenth century was indeed qualified by several influences that did not live easily with one another: the German influence, which stressed pure research and disinterested scholarship; the land-grant tradition, emphasizing community service and applied research; and the normal-school conception, which emphasized practical preparation for teaching. These different emphases have been in relatively continuous competition, and have posed difficult problems of preference to university departments and schools of education, which have, characteristically, vacillated among them over the years. Each of the three emphases has, moreover, undergone significant changes of various sorts, and they have occupied differing relative positions at various times in the history of the Harvard Graduate School of Education, as elsewhere. Yet we may, at the present time, clearly discern three corresponding elements in the operations of our school: programs of pure research and scholarship relating to education; programs of applied research and development involving field relations to various localities; and programs for the training of teachers, counselors, administrators, and other school professionals. Through pure research and scholarship, the School is linked to the academic disciplines; through applied and field work, it is linked to the interests of technology and the practical problems of actual communities; through training, it is linked to the standards and outlook of professional practice. The implicit conception of the study of education, as embodied in these various activities of the School, is indeed a broad one. It enables the School to identify itself as a meeting place of theory and practice, scholarship and social concerns.

We have remarked that a particular strength of the study of education in a university setting is its capacity for developing and sustaining such a broad conception. For in a university setting, such study, with its natural links to practice, has access also to the primary sources of science and scholarship as well as to the processes of mind and method by which such sources are continually replenished. Yet it is at least logically conceivable that such a conception is inferior to some alternative that might be proposed. Let us then analyze certain competing conceptions as to the general orientation of educational study in a university.

ALTERNATIVE ORIENTATIONS

It might be argued, to begin with, that the very existence of an independent graduate school of education is unwarranted, that the effort to form a broad conception of educational study as the basis of an institutional unit of the university had best be abandoned in favor of a deliberate fragmentation of such study and its absorption by other branches of the university. The various scholarly and research disciplines now represented at the Harvard Graduate School of Education could well, it might be thought, be returned to the several arts and sciences departments with which they are naturally affiliated and could continue, from there, to apply themselves to the sphere of education. The preparation of practitioners is a function that might also, in certain respects, be allocated to departments (for example, guidance to psychology or social relations, and teachers' methods courses to the various subject departments) and, in other respects, be made the province of a small interdepartmental committee (for instance, a committee to administer practice teaching and supervise the satisfaction of certification requirements). Such an arrangement, it might be pointed out, has an obvious superiority over the present one in point of economy of effort and money. The enormous energies required to organize, staff, and administer a graduate professional school would no longer need to be expended. The academic faculty, in entering parent departments, would no longer need to develop the special and dangerously isolated careers required by work in a professional-school environment. Interest in education would, moreover, be diffused through all of the University rather than being localized in a separate school. In sum, the strength of a broad and unified orientation to the study of education is gained at a great price: it involves the existence of a separate school. The University could discharge its responsibilities to education (so it might be concluded) in a much more economical way by splintering the study of education and reassigning the fragments.

Such a plan seems to us fatally defective for a variety of reasons. It would utterly destroy the opportunities for continuous confrontations between educationally relevant academic specialties, educational technology, professional practice, and the living problems of school and community. Such confrontations constitute the major channel through which the research and scholarship of the University are tied to the practical enterprises of men. To destroy this channel would doubtless result in economies, but it would just as surely prevent the University from properly fulfilling its responsibilities.

To abolish the School would effectively remove the University from engagement with the profession as well as from any serious enterprise of professional training. Such training simply cannot be properly conducted by one or two designated persons or by a small committee of the Faculty of Arts and Sciences, nor can such a committee command the requisite energy and range for maintaining relations with schools and school people. To fragment the School and absorb it into the departments would, moreover, change the whole quality of the undertaking. In the arts and sciences framework, where the dominant ethos is that of advanced research and scholarship, the outlook of professional education would be relegated to a lower rank. Nor is it clear that the departments would welcome the newer responsibilities that such an arrangement would envisage for them, quite apart from the question whether they are equipped to discharge these responsibilities effectively. It is unlikely that even the natural applications of the scholarly and research disciplines to education would be adequately fostered by the departments alone, much less that methods courses for teachers would be seriously undertaken; it is, in our opinion, fantastic to imagine that abolition of the School would diffuse educational interest throughout the University. Nor would there be a provision of opportunity for conversation and cooperative work between specialists separated by departmental walls, even though they might be severally interested in educational applications. Without the School, finally, there could be no coherent and independent policy of staffing, of recruitment of students, or of long-term research planning, nor would there be room for independent administrative initiative for which the concerns of education were primary. The full power of the University would, in short, fail to be adequately concentrated on the business of education, and the University, in its turn, would be deprived of the stimulation afforded by engagement with educational practice.

Consider now a second alternative to the orientation of the School, which presently embraces research, scholarship, applied work, and professional training under its broad conception of the study of education. This alternative is represented by the notion of an advanced-research institute having as its sole function the development of basic research on the educational process. In particular, it would abjure the tasks of formal teaching and professional training, though it might of course provide research training and sophistication for younger scholars, who would be attached to it for shorter or longer periods. The argument for such an alternative is that it represents a development that would be of undoubted value to the field, and that it is the sort of enterprise that could be carried through especially well at an independent, research-oriented university. The responsibilities of the various institutions throughout the country concerned with education are by no means equivalent; it is, in fact, of great importance for the field at large that special capabilities be emphasized and heightened rather than wasted in a foolish attempt at conformity. Because of Harvard's research strength and its capacity to attract scholars of distinction, it should, so the argument runs, devote itself to the formation of an institute for basic educational research, and leave the domains of professional training and applied work to other agencies. Such a commitment by the University would raise the standing of education throughout the land: it would foster the development of a research elite devoted to education, press for the solution of outstanding theoretical problems, improve the quality of current research work, raise the prestige of research in the eyes of the profession and so enable more thorough dissemination of research findings, and strengthen the position of education as a topic of the University's concern.

Although these considerations seem to us indeed to support the abstract conception of a research institute devoted to education, they do not provide an equally convincing case for reorganizing our school *as* such an institute. This alternative in fact suffers from the defect of the previous one: it destroys the University's engagement with the profession and breaks the link between research and practice. Indeed, in surrendering the teaching and training functions altogether, it departs from the pattern of other professional schools and introduces a relatively isolated foreign body within the University, cutting its natural ties even with the academic departments in allied fields. The argument upon which it rests, moreover, underestimates the importance of teaching and training to the research enterprise itself. An emphasis on research is not merely compatible with, but is actively nourished by, the presence of younger scholars and the need to teach them what is known and to train them to seek what is not known. The University's research capability is thus, in our view, not dissipated, but strengthened, by its intimate connection with teaching. Its research excellence gives it, furthermore, the special opportunity of incorporating professional training and technological development within a research context. Such incorporation serves to improve the whole variety of significant educational positions, and hence to improve the quality of practice. To cut application and professional training away from pure research would ensure the failure of the University to focus fully upon educational endeavors; it would prevent the University from developing highly trained educational workers needed in various significant posts throughout the land. An *exclusive* commitment to basic research by the University would be likely to have serious negative effects upon the field.

We have considered the abolition of the School and its replacement by a research institute. Suppose now, as a less radical third alternative, the retention of the present structure of the School, but with exclusive emphasis on the academic disciplines and their applications to education. The special research capabilities of the University would here again be salient, and much of the previous argument for an exclusive research commitment would carry over to this more moderate proposal. Furthermore, the continuation of the teaching function, and the stress on doctoral programs rather than professional training at the master's level, represent clear advantages over the idea of a research institute. Moreover, training would not be wholly given up. It is specifically the training of school practitioners that would be surrendered, that is, the preparation of teachers for the lower schools, of counselors, administrators, and other school professionals. The training of research experts and of professors capable of applying the academic disciplines to education and prepared to staff positions in schools of education would, on the other hand, be strengthened and expanded. There is hardly any question that such training is of the first importance for the improvement of the field at large, nor is there any question that a university such as Harvard is especially well equipped to sustain such a training effort. Academic departments have not themselves performed this function, but the School already has a strong tradition in this direction that could easily be expanded and developed as the main emphasis of its operations. As contrasted with the training of teachers for the lower schools, such an alternative as is now envisaged would be likely to have much greater long-term influence on the field.

What this argument takes as its positive goal seems to us surely of the highest importance. The application of the major disciplines to education has not been carried nearly far enough, nor is it something that can be left either to academic departments themselves or to those schools of education that are, of necessity, burdened with the primary duty of preparing teachers in large numbers for the lower schools. Without well-trained academicians with a major commitment to working on educational problems and to staffing professorial positions within schools of education, the preparation of teachers throughout the country loses primary contact with the disciplines, and educational research and scholarship falter.

Nevertheless, these considerations do not support the conclusion that the School should take as its exclusive function the application of the academic disciplines to education. To be sure, the preparation of school practitioners at the master's level cannot compete in potential influence with the training of professors of education. But there are professorial positions of significance that do not represent primarily the application of the academic disciplines, and there are important educational careers for which training at the doctoral level is desirable that are not professorships. Administration, counseling, school psychology, curriculum, and supervision are all fields in which doctoral programs are feasible and in which there are positions of high influence both of a professorial and of a nonprofessorial sort. Nor can we, in an exclusive concern with potential influence, altogether ignore the problems of preparing teachers, for teaching is a foundation of our whole undertaking. To relinquish serious involvement with these fields, and with still others of the "clinical" or practitioners' type, is to thwart the fruitful confrontation between them and the academic disciplines. It is to limit the power of the University to affect the educational enterprise at all levels of which it is capable.

As we have already stressed, the perspective of the practitioner is essential for the development of research and scholarship itself if research and scholarship are to be seriously applied to education. The University's strength lies, surely, in research and scholarship, but if this strength is to be brought to bear profitably on human affairs, it must seek, and not shun, opportunities for significant engagement with practice. The proper course is to incorporate in the work of the School not simply the points of view of people trained by way of the academic disciplines, but also those of people schooled in community, clinic, and school as well as those of persons whose primary allegiance is not to disciplinary research but rather to applied research centered on some practical problem area. The primary planning requirement, we believe, is a sense of balance and wholeness—an appreciation of the many voices that need to be heard in significant discourse on educational matters.

Considerations such as these are decisive in evaluating still other orientations that might be envisaged for the School. The suggestion, for example, that the School be exclusively oriented to the doctoral training of practitioners is just as defective as the alternative just considered in that it cuts the tie between practice and theory. Furthermore, it fails to capitalize upon the University's evident academic power, naively trusting to the departments to develop significant educational applications of the disciplines and ignoring the need for a direct attack upon the development of applied academic programs. The alternative suggestion that the School take as its primary task the development of model teacher preparation programs has the same defects in addition to others. The relative impact of such a course on the field at large, as compared with a major commitment to doctoral programs, seems likely to be small. True, the influence of a primary emphasis on preparing teachers would depend not merely on the numbers of teachers graduated, but also on the degree to which model training ideas were taken up by other training institutions. But influence of the latter type does not require that our school take the preparation of teachers as its exclusive, or even primary, task; it is sufficient that one part of its energies be devoted to teacher preparation. It is also important to bear in mind two further aspects of any serious program to improve the preparation of teachers. One is the need to develop critical research into, and evaluation of, teaching processes and the training of teachers. The other is the need to train professors who will staff positions in schools of education that prepare large numbers of teachers. Both these needs seem clearly to demand the commitment of independent universities with research capabilities and a genuine concern for the quality of teacher preparation throughout the country. Both indicate, moreover, a level of commitment that goes far beyond the initiation of model programs of teacher preparation.

The suggestion, finally, that the School adopt an orientation primarily of direct service to the field has very little to recommend it. Such an orientation would squander the University's power to bring advanced research and scholarly illumination to bear on education, and it would divert the University from the important doctoral responsibilities outlined above. Service, in relatively direct forms, certainly has a place within the scope of the School. In engagement with school and clinical facilities for training purposes, we accept a service role to a lesser or greater degree as integral to our training efforts. Further, such practical engagement by the School is essential not only for training but also for the advancement of knowledge. Nevertheless, it is advanced training and the advancement of knowledge that are central to our task and purpose, and it is through these that we hope primarily to render service by developing increased understanding and providing professional leadership. Put another way, the proper service for us to aim at is not the provision of answers to relatively local and immediate problems of practice, or the fulfillment of advisory or personnel needs, as these needs are defined by existing agencies in the field. Rather, we need to strive to serve by developing fundamental ideas, principles of general application, and operational and technological innovations with significant range, and by graduating persons capable of providing educational leadership by virtue of their ideas, training, and professional abilities. To serve appropriately, the University must earn the right to lead.

PRINCIPLE OF CONTEXT

It is time to draw various threads together, to crystallize the several practical principles implicit in our assessment of alternative orientations, and in so doing to make our own recommendations plain. We have recognized, first of all, what might be called a principle of context, which directs us to conceive the study of education in light of the special features of the setting in which it is to be pursued. A university setting, we feel, provides special opportunities for linking pure learning with the practical endeavors of men; it offers the promise of deepening and broadening professional training by incorporating it within a climate of research and scholarship; it provides a channel by which advanced knowledge and critical methods can be brought to bear on educational undertakings; and it brings to the independent life of research and scholarship the continuing stimulation of practice. Such special opportunities pose special responsibilities for independent universities, which are not constrained by the duty to devote themselves primarily to teacher preparation. If these universities fail in such responsibilities, their failure is likely to be reflected in innumerable ways through its adverse effect on the quality of educational thought and the depth of professional training.

In planning for our school, we need to keep such considerations in the forefront of our thinking. The School is part of the University, and its special intellectual potential, technological and clinical as well as academic, depends in large part upon its being part of the University. There is no point in its mounting pro-

grams that could just as well be carried out elsewhere while ne
glecting the special responsibilities that flow from Harvard's
strength. Conversely, there is every reason to develop the peculiar
opportunities that membership in the University offers. As one
of Harvard's professional schools, the Graduate School of Edu
cation should think of itself as the University proper, focused
upon the field of education. Its special challenge is to identify
and feed into the center of the University the live problems o
school and community, and, concurrently, to concentrate all
relevant energies of the University upon education and its mo
tivating ideas and hopes.

A broad conception of the School's work is clearly required to
sustain such an effort of mediation between university and social
practice. It is especially pertinent to the field of education a
distinct from other professions—and professional analogies, use
ful in other respects, may here mislead. We do not, in contrast
with the lawyer, for example, have a special set of texts and
interpretations that can be largely cultivated in relative isolation
nor do we have a characteristic set of technological tools or re
stricted subject matter. Education is as broad as all of culture
it must turn outward and incorporate the life of culture and the
mind in all its forms rather than build a narrow and defensive
haven for itself. But this does not imply that it does not have its
own important work to do. To link a university's realm of theory
with the practical endeavors of education is a full-scale and
serious undertaking, and requires the structure and autonomy o
a graduate school for its proper execution. But such autonomy
should result neither in isolation nor complacency. It should
rather, issue in broad and secure relations with the rest of the
university, in the initiation of multiple dialogues with its other
schools, in a continuing effort at critical self-evaluation and self
improvement, and in the attempt to create a pervading atmos
phere of intellectual excitement in programs of training, research
and scholarship.

PRINCIPLE OF BALANCE

A second principle we have earlier acknowledged is a principle of balance, stressing the importance of building into the School's life the diversity of outlooks that alone can provide opportunities for significant intellectual tension, confrontation, and growth. We have emphasized the linking of research and scholarship with the realm of practice. But we must avoid thinking of these as simple and abstract opposites represented, on the one hand, by the ivory-tower scientist or historian and, on the other hand, by the hard-working, practical classroom teacher. The relevant diversity can, in fact, be specified in greater detail. On the side of research and scholarship, we must try to allow not only for a variety of disciplines but for a multiplicity of modes, running from a primary motivation by disciplinary concerns, which bear on education only in an indirect and long-term manner, to a primary concern with applied, technological, clinical, or field studies centering quite directly on practical problems. On the side of practice, we must reckon not only with the problems of the teacher, but with the concerns of educational planning and administration, the issues of guidance, counseling, and school psychology, the complexities of curriculum and supervision, and the changing world of educational technology.

To sustain such diversity, we must, moreover, enter into different sorts of relations as a school. We must relate ourselves not only to the learned societies and the academic departments through our basic research and scholarship, but to the profession and its subgroups through our training programs and applied work, and to schools, clinics, and communities through field associations. These multiple relations are, we believe, essential to the health of the School. They provide the opportunity for concrete influences to flow from the highest reaches of theory to the most detailed issues of practice, and back again. Through the intimate jostling of the several disciplinary points of view with one another and with the outlooks of the practitioners, a condition is created whereby ideas may be tested through mutual criticism and competition, and where the lessons of experience may be brought to bear. Such a condition makes it possible for the problems of practice to reverberate into the center of the University, as well as for the ideas and methods of this center to find significant scope for application.

PRINCIPLE OF INFLUENCE

A third principle we have employed is a principle of influence, which directs us to shape the work of the School so as to maximize its fundamental and long-term impact. This is not a principle of smug self-assurance about the rightness of our beliefs, but rather a principle of responsibility for the proper use of the University's resources of research and scholarship. In commanding such resources, our school is obligated to employ them in the most effective manner, to provide scholarly perspective, to cultivate logical habits of criticism and evaluation, to advance our knowledge of educational processes and our understanding of their social contexts, to improve the state of professional practice, and to provide high-level training to those capable of profiting from it. Such effective use of the resources of the University requires that we reject a primary commitment to meeting the current needs of practice as generated by existing conditions, that we shun a basic involvement with relatively isolated or transient concerns, and that we avoid incoherent lines of development contingent mainly upon current fads or available financial backing. It requires rather that we concentrate on our proper long-term and fundamental goals of advancing knowledge, providing training of high quality, enlightening our understanding of pressing human problems, and improving the professional art.

The principle of influence is by no means incompatible with

applied work. It means only that, in application, our work must be designed to yield generalizable truths and operational devices. It means that our clinical and field involvements, however worthwhile, should not be ends in themselves, but means for the attainment of new levels of general proficiency, for finding significant facts concerning human nature and schooling, for developing new and generalizable modes of training. Rather than following the lead of existing practice, we need to accept the challenge to provide leadership, based upon new ideas systematically developed and critically tested, to the various fields of practice.

Such a challenge to leadership is particularly relevant at the present time, for tremendous forces of change are at work. The continued growth of the field of education, the new global involvements of universities, the increasing educational commitment of government, the explosion of communications technology, and the fantastic expansion of education outside the classroom—these developments show that it would be folly to look to the past, or even the present scene, to conceive ourselves as training graduates to fill specific jobs in an enterprise that can be counted on to stand still and wait for them. The need is for universities to be inventive in defining the future before it is upon us: to create new fundamental ideas adequate to the times, while fostering and disseminating the old virtues of critical thought in dealing with them. We cannot, in short, think of the School of Education as simply training functionaries for an ongoing system. We need rather to relate the School boldly to the strangenesses and opportunities of the new world—to encourage it to create new patterns and roles of endeavor, to educate the public and raise the standards of the profession, while holding fast to the tried values of critical humanism that form the core of the University's life.

What then, in sum, do we recommend for orientation? The guiding conception of educational study to which our school has in recent years been committed seems to us fundamentally sound, its broad interpretation of education superior to any alternative that we have considered. The policy of cultivating diverse approaches and outlooks seems to us healthy, and indeed essential for continued health. Such features of the School need, however to be strengthened and further developed; they require our continuing efforts to support and expand their application in all phases of the School's work, for they represent ideals that we have, unfortunately, hardly realized fully in practice. We believe moreover, that the attempt to provide advanced scholarship training, and professional leadership is of the first importance in the future orientation of the School, and requires a re-evaluation of its main priorities. In Part II, we consider some fundamental practical problems posed by these conclusions, and propose general instrumentalities by which they may be met.

PART II

GENERAL PROBLEMS AND PROPOSALS

The picture we have drawn so far represents the Graduate School of Education, ideally, as a vital part of the University whose special task it is to relate the content, methods, and values of research and scholarship to the concerns of educational practice, not only in order to advance knowledge and to enlighten judgment, but also to improve the professional art. We have conceived the School, accordingly, as providing common ground for a multiplicity of theoretical and practical outlooks, and as being linked outwardly to other schools in the University, to the profession, and to live problems of school and community. We have, finally, pictured the School as making maximally efficient use of its resources in concentrating upon the fundamental theoretical problems of the field and in striving equally for general and long-term amelioration of educational practice.

Such an ideal picture makes serious demands of the school that tries to realize it. We shall, in this part, focus our attention on three major problems. There is, first of all, the perennial problem of ensuring that the School's major priorities are adjusted to achieve maximum efficiency and influence. This we shall call the problem of priorities. There is, second, the problem of organization, that is, the problem of so organizing the School as to achieve maximum coherence as well as a proper balance among the diverse aspects of its work. Finally, and most difficult, is the problem of integration: how to incorporate integrating principles and devices into the life of the School so as to counteract the centrifugal forces generated by its unusual diversity.

We shall outline several recommendations that constitute, in our opinion, a reasonable response to the above three problems, at least as they involve the School as a whole. Our concern here is, then, with general instrumentalities to meet problems affecting the entire School; our specific proposals for more particular issues will be reserved for Part III.

PRIORITIES

Turning first to the question of priorities, we feel that a considerable shift in the School's effort is called for, in the direction of a greater emphasis on doctoral training. The strength of the School's resources clearly lies in its capacity for supporting advanced work. To devote our energies to the project of producing large numbers of teachers for the lower schools seems to us an inefficient use of our capabilities. In the fall of 1964, for example we enrolled 234 students as candidates for the Ed.D., and 433 students as candidates for master's degrees, 80 of whom were working for the Master of Education in Elementary Education and 276 of whom were registered as candidates for the Master of Arts in Teaching, which prepares teachers for secondary schools. We recommend a substantial reduction in the number of master's degree candidates. We further recommend that the Committee on Academic Policy supervise this reduction in accordance with specific plans to be solicited from those responsible for the several programs, which may, in fact, differ in their needs and capabilities. (The "areas," to be described in the next section would perhaps be the appropriate agencies for developing these plans.)

The bulk of our efforts should thus be devoted to doctoral training, and the general climate of the School accordingly be shifted in the direction of advanced studies. We propose that the Ed.M. in scholarly or disciplinary fields and the general Ed.M. be given up, or else radically restricted, since they are at best stepping stones to doctoral study and do not in themselves represent a clear and "terminal" level of professional competence. The exploratory function that they sometimes fulfill for students who are as yet undecided about doctoral study can be equally well fulfilled by graduate study without matriculation for a degree. The presumption should then be, as it is generally understood to be in the arts and sciences, that in the academic or scholarly fields the master's degree is insignificant, and that it is instead the doctor's degree that sets operative goals and standards.

On the other hand, we are by no means proposing that all master's degree programs be abandoned, nor are we suggesting that the School altogether relinquish the task of preparing teachers. We are mindful of the desirable features of our past efforts in teacher preparation (for example, with the Master of Arts in Teaching) and of what have generally been considered their beneficial effects on the field at large. We are also convinced that the problems of teacher preparation are essential ingredients of the work of any school of education, and that they provide a critical link with professional practice. Moreover, many of our best doctoral students have come from the ranks of our master's degree graduates in the professional (or so-called clinical) areas. It seems to us, furthermore, that clinical master's degree programs can be so designed as to represent a coherent and relatively "terminal" level of professional competence, and that a constructive effort to carry through such a design on a relatively small scale would both fall within our capacities and promise to contribute substantially to the improvement of professional standards in the field. Finally, we believe that suitable clinical master's programs might well be integrated into doctoral programs in the clinical fields.

Therefore we are recommending not an abandonment but rather a quantitative reduction of our commitment to master's degree programs, together with a concurrent effort to work out a coherent design for programs leading to professional practice in the schools. We shall outline our proposals for such a design in

Part III. Here our concern is only to specify the major priorities that seem to us advisable for the School to adopt. The course we propose would facilitate a more deliberate and experimental attack upon the issues of professional training for school practice; it would also channel the School's major efforts into doctoral training.

It is doctoral training that appears to us to have the greatest potential for fundamental and long-term influence upon the field of education. It is this training, also, that poses the most challenging current problem of professional definition, namely, the problem of working out a productive combination of fundamental studies providing advanced training for a new variety of careers in educational practice, all to be informed by intellectual values, technical proficiency, and clinical awareness. We have here a challenge to strengthen the power and raise the standards of the profession, as well as to improve the quality of the currently expanding educational endeavor, by training able and intellectual professionals for key posts in schools, communities, universities, industry, government, communications, planning, and research. The problem, as we see it, is not to multiply doctoral programs aimed at these several posts, but rather to work out a new conception of advanced professional training to anticipate new forms of educational responsibility, which are developing at an explosive rate. At the same time, we need to maintain and strengthen our doctoral programs for pure research and scholarship so that we may prepare graduates to serve in schools of education as professors applying academic disciplines to education. Without such a concurrent effort, the endeavor to develop advanced practitioners' programs is likely to lack substance and balance. The general task of the School, then, as we see it, is to concentrate its efforts in programs on the doctoral level and to work out a rational set of programs both for advanced professional practice and for advanced research and scholarship on subjects of educational concern.

Partly for reasons similar to the above, we also recommend

adding a postdoctoral level of study to the operational structure of the School. We shall indicate in greater detail in the next part how we conceive such a level. At this point, we wish simply to state, in connection with the question of general priorities, that we believe it would be desirable for the School to develop some form of postdoctoral activity on a relatively small scale. Such activity would capitalize upon the School's considerable resources for advanced study, and would be likely to stimulate the general progress of learning in areas relevant to education; it would also enable the School to develop new associations with and among established educational scholars from this land and abroad, and in so doing help to raise the standards of educational discussion in the public, as well as the professional, community.

ORGANIZATION

Let us turn now to the problem of organization, the problem of achieving a balanced and coherent structure. Such a structure, were it attained, would also help to integrate the School, to make its priorities explicit, and to render its operations more efficient. What, then, is the proper way to effect a balanced articulation of the School's elements? There is surely no single, exclusive answer to this question, but the need to provide a greater degree of structural coherence has become increasingly urgent in recent years. We thus venture to recommend a mode of organization that seems promising to us and worth trying, on an experimental basis.

Before outlining our proposal, however, it might be well to note certain background points. The sort of structure we are here concerned with is neither the administrative structure nor the faculty committee structure, which is designed to carry forward the essential official business of the School (and is, in any event, subject to the dean's prerogative, with the approval of appropriate University authorities). Nor are we concerned at this point with the structure of individual program requirements or projects. We are rather concerned with relatively natural groupings of faculty sharing common intellectual interests and professional commitments.

The Harvard Graduate School of Education does not have formal departments, but only programs and groups of related programs with associated faculty advisers. The ethos of the School is, moreover, opposed to departmentalization. Undoubtedly an underlying reason for such opposition has been the desire to avoid departmental imperialism, interdepartmental strife, and rampant scholarly specialization. A more salient reason, perhaps, has been the desire to create a "circular" pattern of studies appropriate to a professional school, and different from the "linear" disciplinary pattern characterizing arts and sciences departments. The intent has been for this projected pattern of studies to center on the problems of education, employing whatever disciplinary or practical approaches seemed relevant and promising, with the hope that, out of the cross relation of approaches with a common educational center, would grow a new and stronger professional spirit. Opposition to departmentalization has been largely based on the wish to facilitate such cross relation. Such motivation is evident also in the way doctoral requirements are currently set: the doctoral candidate's supervisory committees are all composed of members with diverse academic affiliations, to ensure that the student shall develop his ideas not simply for his academic in-group, but for a general audience of educational scholars with varying perspectives.

There is, it must be admitted, considerable weight to these antidepartmental considerations, and considerable merit in the attempt to develop an organization peculiarly appropriate to a professional school. Yet success in completely avoiding departmentalization depends, among other things, upon size. With a relatively small school, such avoidance may still leave open essential lines of communication and allow effective lines of authority and initiative to remain visible. With a small school, furthermore, decisions may be crystallized in a relatively informal fashion, and policy may grow with a minimum of explicit procedure. The fact is, however, that our school has grown significantly over the past fifteen years. The data recorded in Appendix D show our expansion in various dimensions during this period.

In addition, the School has, in this time, added the Laboratory for Research in Instruction, the Center for Studies in Education and Development, the Center for Research in Careers, the Center for Research and Development on Educational Differences; has developed SUPRAD (School and University Program for Research and Development), the Harvard-Newton, Harvard-Lexington, and Harvard-Boston summer programs; worked with COPI (Committee on Programmed Instruction) and NEEDS (New England Education Data Systems); and undertaken a project of several years' duration involving the operation of an American-style comprehensive high school in Nigeria. Faculty appointments linking the School with the Faculty of Arts and Sciences have been made during this period that relate the School specifically to the Departments of History, Philosophy, Social Relations, Psychology, Linguistics, and Mathematics.

The result of such growth has been that we have lost the effective capacity to operate primarily in informal ways, but have lacked the explicit structure to channel more formal arrangements. The antidepartmental ethos has, moreover, made it difficult for us to recognize our actual growth, and difficult also to admit that reforms were needed. We have thus continued to tell ourselves and others that we are small and informal, while allowing the actual processes of our decision making to develop in complex and haphazard ways, and without official acknowledgment of their existence. The operative structure has, in consequence, become more obscure with the years both to our students and to our faculty. Lines of authority have become blurred, communication has suffered, and faculty initiative has become confused.

It is in this context that our organizational recommendation needs to be understood. We shall first outline this recommendation and then present some of its main features and hoped-for advantages, as we see them. The proposal is to form not departments but quasi-departmental units representing faculty groupings, to be called "areas." We envisage six such areas, three of them "disciplinary" in character, and three applied or "clinical" in character. The three disciplinary areas are those of the humanities, the social sciences, and psychology; the three clinical areas are those of administration, guidance, and teaching. Each area is to have as primary affiliates, on a relatively continuing basis, members of the faculty whose work falls within its rubric. It will, in addition, have as visiting affiliates, on a variable basis, those faculty members for whom it represents a secondary identification as well as those who wish simply to gain an insight into its operations, methods, and problems in furthering their self-education.

The primary affiliates of the six areas, as we estimate the matter, are as follows. For the humanities, faculty members representing history and philosophy; for the social sciences, faculty members representing sociology, economics, political science, and anthropology; for psychology, faculty members representing various of the psychological specialties, including measurement; for administration, faculty members representing the School's programs in administrative training; for guidance, faculty members representing the School's training programs in guidance, counseling, and school psychology; and for teaching, faculty members representing the School's training programs in teacher preparation, curriculum, supervision, and research in instruction. Visiting affiliates will include those faculty members who see themselves as naturally belonging to more than one area in the nature of their work (for example, a psychologist who is greatly involved in training programs in the guidance area), and also those who want to find out more about the work of their colleagues in a given area, even though they are not themselves identified with it professionally.

We suggest a relatively easygoing method for working out affiliations of both sorts—a process of discussion between faculty member and dean. But certain general policies might well be encouraged: the rotation of visiting affiliations and perhaps also, though much less frequently, of primary affiliations where appropriate; the choice by every faculty member of one primary and one visiting affiliation each year, with the presumption that for many (perhaps most) members, one of these will be disciplinary, the other clinical; the spread of each disciplinary area's visiting affiliations among all clinical areas, and vice versa.

We recommend that each area have a chairman appointed by the dean for a three-year term, normally on a rotating basis. Our suggestion is that each area chairman call monthly meetings of his group during the academic year. There would be a certain set of relatively internal matters to be handled by each area, and we imagine these to fall essentially within the responsibility of primary affiliates. Such matters include, for example, the planning of course offerings for the coming year; the organization of those basic "service" courses that are given in the area; the search for, and recommendation of, candidates for junior appointments; the representation of the area's views to the School's administration, to other areas, and to faculty committees; the orientation of new faculty members and students within the area; and the guidance and evaluation of students. Aside from these matters, however, we propose that each area provide, for both primary and visiting affiliates, the continuing opportunity for free discussion and exchange of ideas on intellectual, program, and policy concerns that are germane to the work of the area. Such opportunity for discussion should enable faculty members to test new ideas relating to an area in the informal but critical atmosphere provided by circles of their own colleagues. It should also enable them to benefit from the regular confrontation of diverse views from without, as well as within, their own areas.

It seems to us that the areas provide a balanced structure that conveys and implements the basic commitments of the School. The intent to tie research and scholarship to practice is clearly signaled by the inclusion of three disciplinary as well as three clinical areas; the fundamental importance of both disciplines and clinical practice in the work of the School is emphasized by its very structure. Moreover, the disciplinary and clinical areas are so construed as to embrace a significant diversity of concerns. The problems of practice are represented not only by the teaching area, with its primary emphasis on cognitive processes, subject matter, and methods of instruction, but also by the guidance area, whose primary concern is with individual development, growth, and choice, and by the area of administration, whose main interests are school operation, educational planning, and public policy. Disciplinary research and scholarship embrace not only studies of a historical and philosophical character in the humanities area, but also scientific studies of cognition, learning, and development in the psychology area, and investigations of society, school, and culture in the area of the social sciences.

The breadth of the School's conception of the study of education is specified in such a way that distinctive analytic levels and methodological perspectives may have a place in its intellectual life. Thus the processes of individual learning and development are studied in the area of psychology, while the social and institutional contexts of such processes are the focus of the area of social sciences. Whereas these two areas strive for general explanatory models of their subject matter, the historian of the humanities area approaches the same subject matter with an eye for the individual developments that comprise it and an appreciation of the unique constellations of factors by which such developments are qualified. And while all these foregoing studies are primarily descriptive in intent and character, the philosophical studies of the humanities area are, rather, concerned with critical as well as normative approaches—with analysis of central concepts and assumptions as well as with evaluation of varieties of educational purpose.

In the clinical areas, too, differing perspectives are represented. We have in the teaching area, for example, the cluster of characteristic approaches of teacher, cognitive psychologist, subject-matter expert, curriculum designer, and applied researcher, all converging on school learning. In the guidance area, we have another cluster, where the approaches of personality theorist, clinical and child psychologist, diagnostician, counselor, career researcher, and guidance worker are brought to bear on the problems of individual choice, growth, and mental health. Finally, in the administration area, we have the cluster of approaches of administrator, economist, sociologist, political scientist, and educational planner, all centering on the operation of schools and school systems.

Furthermore, the clinical areas clearly express the School's commitment to the training of advanced practitioners, whereas the disciplinary areas express its equal commitment to training scholars capable of bringing the scientific and humanistic disciplines to bear on education. It is of the utmost importance, however, to recognize that the simple contrast between practice and theory is not the intended underlying contrast between the clinical and disciplinary areas, for in the clinical areas there are also research and scholarship, and in the disciplinary areas there is application to practice. What is involved is, first of all, a form of organization: the disciplines in each of the clinical areas converge on a specific set of practical problems, whereas in the disciplinary areas they follow an individual and autonomous course, with forms of application not specified in advance. Second, the clinical areas, unlike the disciplinary areas, have as one of their basic commitments the task of graduating professionals who will have careers of action and practical decision.

The recommended areas seem to us to provide the sort of additional structure whose need has become increasingly evident. They specify certain responsibilities that have until now been indeterminate (course planning, organization of "service courses"), they require area chairmen to perform tasks of administration and leadership hitherto carried out in an informal manner at best, and they create the means for carrying out several important functions in a natural, explicit, and orderly fashion. Thus they enable new faculty members to be properly oriented in an informal and sympathetic manner; provide the opportunity for regular meetings with students and for periodic reviews of their work; offer the stimulus for the formation of coherent lines of area planning and development; constitute a natural forum for the discussion of new program ideas and policy innovations; and facilitate faculty communication across program boundaries, thus being likely to encourage greater faculty participation in matters of academic policy and curriculum in the School. The areas are, moreover, likely to be able to ascertain systematically their own long-term needs and to offer improved representation of such needs to the rest of the School. Finally, they can provide representative counsel to the dean on matters of importance.

Structurally, the areas constitute an intermediate level between administration and individual faculty member, and the existence of such a level is, in our view, likely to render their mutual relations easier. "Service courses" (those designed for students outside the specialty) can, for example, be seen as the obligation of the areas, and not necessarily as individual faculty assignments. Administrative criticism, direction, and negotiation can be pointed more easily toward area responsibilities, while the faculty member has always available the society of his area colleagues, who will offer him both support and criticism in the working out of his role within the School.

Perhaps most important is the prospect of increased faculty discussion, which the areas will foster. With the extreme diversity characteristic of the School, special provisions for encouraging discussion are extremely significant. We hope that this will be the areas' greatest contribution, thus furthering the integrating tendencies in the School's life.

INTEGRATION

We turn now to the problem of integration: providing those principles and devices that are capable of binding the School together, despite its enormous diversity. To some extent, we have already dealt with this problem. In recommending a reduction of commitment to master's degree programs, as well as an intensification of doctoral training, and in proposing, also, the addition of a postdoctoral level to the operations of the School, we are in effect suggesting that the School's dominant emphasis be made that of advanced study and training. We hope that such a dominant emphasis will permeate all aspects of School life, with an integrative effect—that it will introduce, throughout, a sense of the fascination of research into frontier problems, an appreciation of research technique and sound intellectual method, an understanding of the contexts and dilemmas of advanced educational practice, and a zest for professional leadership through service of high quality.

Our area recommendation will also, we hope, have a substantial integrating effect. For not only does it bring to the fore as the two main structural foci of the School the disciplines and the areas of clinical practice, but also it sets up the conditions for coherent area development and cross-area conversations on a continuing basis. Such features of the recommendation are fundamental to our notion of proper integration, and are thus worth further comment.

We are, in effect, here rejecting the notion of a special science of education as a basis for integration. Such a notion has, on occasion, been looked to as the basis for an independent status for schools of education, or, at the least, as providing the common core of the work of such schools. Such hopes for a science of education seem to us to rest on quicksand. Detailed negative considerations are put forth in John Walton and James L. Kuethe's recent collection, *The Discipline of Education* (University of Wisconsin, 1963), but a few points may here be noted.

A science is counted by its peculiar ideas, instruments, and procedures, but, most importantly, by its distinctive laws and theories. Education has no such distinctive laws and theories. To be sure, educational phenomena may be studied in a scientific manner, but the current attempts to study education scientifically proceed from a wide variety of directions, and utilize a multiplicity of concepts, procedures, and research styles. It is unlikely in the extreme that they will all coalesce into, or be superseded by, a unified educational science. To the extent, moreover, that any one of these approaches may itself be acknowledged as having the status of a fundamental science, it is in fact inappropriate to think of it as a peculiarly educational science.

On the other hand, any advance in these general approaches is likely to benefit the scientific study of education. It is the latter enterprise, after all, that is, and should be, our basic concern. Whether we have one or many sciences, whether or not any of these is specifically a science of education, is irrelevant to the possibility of studying education in a scientific spirit. And the fact is that this possibility can be, and is being, realized in diverse ways, in accordance with various research models and investigative styles. The autonomy of a school of education is sufficiently supported by the concern to further this whole variety of studies in application to education; it does not in addition require the tenuous hope of a special science of education.

Nor does the concept of educational foundations appeal to us as providing the sort of integration appropriate to a graduate school of education. We have no quarrel with efforts to strengthen the general education of teachers and to relate their work to pressing social problems, such efforts constituting basic motivations of the "foundations approach." Nevertheless, we are skeptical of the attempt to provide an interdisciplinary conglomerate of indispensible educational content. In practice, such an attempt seems to us often to involve the piecing together of results taken from a wide selection of studies and presented in an inspirational vein. In our view, such a piecing together of results, especially with inspirational intent, is likely to overlook the basic differences of approach, method, and level of precision that qualify the diverse results in question. It provides a static synthesis, whereas what is required, most especially in advanced work, is a live and continuing confrontation of investigative approaches with one another and with problems of practice.

Such a confrontation is what we hope will emerge from increased conversation among faculty and students, across areas. Instead of seeking integration through a common science, or through a common body of formulated knowledge, we seek integration, both for our students and our faculty, through common discussions in which both disciplinary and clinical outlooks are represented. Such an approach can, however, succeed only if discussion is serious and thoroughgoing. We propose, then, as a further principle of integration, the strengthening of critical thought and dialogue in all the work of the School. Our impression is that we probably ask our students to read too much and too fast; we ask them to listen passively too much of the time, and to think not nearly enough. We suggest, therefore, a greater attempt to elicit the critical thought, discussion, and reflective writing of students, and an increased experimentation with seminars, case discussion, tutorials, and similar methods.

Integration is not isolation. We seek not a school with jealously guarded walls, but a school that is a meeting place of advanced scholars and enlightened practitioners with a common interest in education. The discussions taking place under its auspices should not separate it from either the University or the profession. They should rather help to strengthen its many ties with other parts of the University, and to link it ever more closely with the problems of practical life and professional improvement.

PART III

SPECIFIC PROPOSALS

In the present part, we shall presuppose the general orientation and the recommendations already set forth, and turn to particular aspects. We shall deal first with programs, next with research, and, finally, with the needs and development of the several areas.

PROGRAMS

The programs we envisage for the Graduate School of Education are of four main types: master's degree programs, doctoral programs, postdoctoral programs, and nondegree institutes. These will be discussed in order.

The master's degree. We have already suggested a reduction of our commitment to master's degree programs, with elimination of academic or "disciplinary" master's degrees, and abandonment, for all practical purposes, of the degree of Master of Education for General Purposes. Concurrently, we have suggested that fresh and intensive consideration be devoted to the design of "clinical" master's degree programs of high quality (for students with or without prior professional experience, but with potential for further advanced training). We present here our proposals regarding the basic structure of such design.

These proposals stem, in large part, from dissatisfaction with our current master's level programs in areas of clinical practice. Our judgment is that one year, of primarily academic work, is definitely inadequate as professional preparation. It does not provide sufficient opportunity for the development of basic proficiency, nor does it encourage the growth of professional identity and strength. Such a year's work therefore represents a deficient sort of preparation for educational practice. Nor do the difficulties reside simply in the shortness of the time or in the remoteness of primarily academic pursuits. Our feeling is that the purely academic elements of current master's programs are not adequately thought through with the purposes of professional practice in mind, and, moreover, that they are insufficiently integrated with one another; there is, furthermore, so much variability in individual program development that the degree of overlapping in individual programs is very small. As a result, the sense of a unifying philosophy is lacking, and the feeling of professional comradeship fails adequately to take hold among students during the period of their master's training.

These comments will not, we hope, be misunderstood. We are opposed neither to academic specialization, to individuality in teaching styles, to research emphases, nor to flexibility. Nor do we yearn for a batch of practical how-to-do-it courses, neatly dovetailed with one another and outfitted with some inspirational philosophy, to be administered rigidly to generations of future students. Professional training in education, as we have repeatedly urged, needs to be incorporated into the wide and free world of culture and intellect that the university represents; it needs always to supplement mere technique with the refinement of critical judgment and the awareness of human values. Yet to say this is by no means to deny the legitimacy of educational practice as a major focus of our teaching, nor does it preclude the recognition that professional training imposes special demands and gives rise to special criteria of relevance. Academic components of such training need to be developed not only with their several autonomous requirements in mind, but also with a view to their joint capacity to enlighten the practitioner's judgment, sharpen his awareness, and heighten his critical sense of the purposes that his performance may realize. Professional practice ought, in short, to provide a broad context of relevance, which qualifies not only the teaching in individual courses at the master's level but also the combined effect of such courses. A sense of design should, moreover, permeate the linking together of such courses in students' programs, providing a common thread in their professional education.

We are dissatisfied also with the clinical components of current master's programs at the School. It is not merely that the quality of our clinical training, such as it is, could be improved, as was urged in several responses to our alumni questionnaires in 1964-65. It is rather that the whole conception and scope of such training seem to us to require radical revision. To prepare a student for teaching on the basis of one year's work, a fraction of which is devoted to apprentice teaching, seems to us simply inadequate. To graduate him at the end of such a year is, furthermore, to abandon him at the critical stage of entry into practice, a stage in which his academic training is being joined to the experience of full clinical responsibility, and in which his personal style of work is being shaped.

We propose, then, a general design in which a new academic sequence is to be meshed with a revised and expanded clinical experience, the whole program to extend beyond the single year. Briefly, we suggest a year's academic residence, preceded by a summer of clinical initiation and followed by up to a year of supervised, paid internship. The academic year would provide for a minimum of two half courses chosen from among history, philosophy, psychology, and sociology (or related courses to be developed by the social sciences area), and would include also a new experimental full course developed on a case and tutorial model and designed to facilitate realistic entry into the educational profession. Full-time supervised practice with pay would be undertaken at the end of the year's residence, but the master's degree would not be awarded until this internship had been satisfactorily completed. The details of the plan are as follows.

(1) The first summer is to be devoted to a clinical or "laboratory" experience, which would serve to introduce students to problems, concepts, and realities of education, in the setting of practice; such a setting might be conceived, for example, after the manner of the Harvard-Newton Summer School. Different varieties of practice, such as teaching and counseling, could be suitably accommodated by such an arrangement, and the work done during the summer would count as the equivalent of two half courses. The summer would set the stage, in the field of practice, for the academic work of the following year. (To maintain the proper level of quality in such summer work, our own faculty would need to provide substantial support in the form of direct participation, *or* in help with suitable arrangements for staffing. The operation as a whole would, of course, require the whole-hearted backing of the School itself.)

(2) Such academic work is to include a minimum of two half courses chosen from among the disciplines of history of education, philosophy of education, psychology of education, and sociology of education (or related courses to be developed by the social sciences area); one full course, Introduction to Education; and four half courses to be designated by the particular program (such as mathematics courses for prospective mathematics teachers, or psychology courses for prospective guidance workers).

The disciplinary options are of great importance, in our opinion. Each discipline puts the practice of education into a general perspective and applies to education a battery of critical methods of analysis. It is supremely important for the professional educator to acquire not merely the pratical skills requisite to his work, but the ability to grasp such work as a subject of intellectual criticism, and the capacity to understand certain of its general ramifications. The four designated disciplinary fields provide a fundamental framework for the understanding of education, its concepts and purposes, its development and social environment, and its underlying mental mechanisms.

We urge the appropriate areas to examine their offerings systematically and to develop sequences suitable for the fulfillment of the disciplinary requirements we have proposed. Such sequences should include general introductory courses, in which fundamental disciplinary methodologies are exemplified in application to topics of relevance to the understanding of education; middle-level courses and seminars, offering more advanced treatments of smaller ranges of topics, and suitable for those with some prior sophistication; and advanced seminars for those with considerable prior background. We expect that there will usually be more than one offering of each type in each appropriate area.

A consequence of our recommendation is the elimination of the system of written appraisal examinations (for the purpose of waiving required courses) that has been in effect. We recognize that no single course is absolutely essential for effective teaching, but we believe that certain minimal sorts of sophistication are highly desirable and indeed essential to a professional conception of educational work. Thus we wish to eliminate the possibility that a student may waive his disciplinary requirements altogether. He has an initial choice of (at least) two disciplinary courses; should he have prior background in any of his chosen disciplines, he has the further possibility of taking a middle-level or a seminar course in the same discipline, after consultation with the instructor and adviser. He has, in other words, the possibility of informally "appraising up but not out." In special circumstances, furthermore, he might be advised to "appraise up" by taking suitable courses in other schools of the University. He might even be allowed to waive one of the disciplinary areas, by special action of the Committee on Degrees, but we expect that such action would be taken very infrequently. In advocating abolition of our present appraisal system, we emphatically do not reject its underlying purpose of providing individually appropriate programs for students. We urge all advisers, in operating under our new proposals, to continue to strive for a maximum of flexibility and intellectual challenge in individual programs, within the limits we have set forth above.

Turning now to the full course, Introduction to Education, we conceive such a course as running throughout the year, and as providing an initiation into the live problems of the educational enterprise. At present, there are several courses in the catalogue with somewhat the same intent, offered by different specialized programs. Our proposal is to use the opportunity for professional initiation as the occasion for a common experience, across specialties. Thus we propose elimination of A-5 (American School: Contemporary Issues in American Education); B-6 (American School: The Social Foundations); C-16 (Principles of Teaching: Supervised Teaching in the Secondary School); C-17 (Administration: Introduction to Administrative Problems in Education); C-18 (Guidance: Principles, Practices, and Organization); C-19 (Elementary Education: Program and Organization of the Elementary School); and C-20 (Secondary Education: Organization, Administration, and Program of the Secondary School), and their replacement by the single course now under discussion.

The course is to be developed experimentally over a considerable period of time by a faculty group headed by the dean. It should emphasize cases and employ a variety of tutorial sections suited to different interests and levels of background. It should incorporate field experiences at schools, clinics, and educationally related facilities of various sorts, and provide contact with processes of teaching, counseling, administration, and policy making at such facilities. It should provide a stimulus to critical observation and evaluation of educational processes and significant opportunity for critical discussion, reading, and (most important) the writing of numerous educational "briefs" and "opinion papers." A more extended individual study might also be required, and a specially designed comprehensive examination might prove to be a desirable culmination. Following a period of experimentation by those responsible for its development, the content and interpretation of this course, as well as its status as a requirement within the total program, would be subject to faculty review.

The four (or perhaps five) half courses left to the individual program are to be used as required by the special demands of the program. Further work in the teaching subject might be advised for prospective teachers, theoretical and clinical work might be designated for counselors; technical, general, individual, and elective courses are all available to fill out any design that seems warranted for the preparation that is the goal of the special program.

(3) The second summer is to be left open, its disposition to be decided by the particular programs. But suitable apprenticeships should, in any event, be planned so that eligible students might undertake them, thus gaining further valuable experience prior to the internship of the second year. A variety of types of apprenticeship should be sought, with independent as well as government agencies, national as well as local.

(4) The second year should provide for a period of supervised clinical internship, with pay, for at least half of the available time (the exact amount to be left to the design of the particular program). The major goal is to provide first-rate supervision, appropriate instruction, criticism, and support during this crucial period, when the "functional translation" of academic preparation into practice is taking place. Such an effort should be supported by development of appropriate clinical professorships and paid supervisory relations with school people. The internship of a new teacher might run through the whole first year of his paid employment; the internship of an experienced teacher might well be shorter, or it might be of a sort different from that represented by his earlier experience, for example, in curriculum development. The important point is that the School maintain its supervisory relation to the student during the postresidence period of internship. It is crucial to the plan that such supervision

be regular, serious, and supplemented with opportunities for seminar meetings with fellow interns and faculty.

An important feature of this plan is that it does not involve simply an extension of the residence period, and therefore does not delay the entry into practice of eager candidates, beyond the one year hitherto required. Yet it extends the supervisory period and the School relationship into the critical period of transition to practice, the period that is, in our view, most widely neglected in clinical training and most in need of improved treatment.

This general design for the master's degree is, in our proposal, to cover all master's degrees offered by the School, including the M.A.T. as well as the Ed.M. An important consequence of this proposal is the abolition of master's programs requiring summer work only. In addition to programs for the preparation of teachers, and of those for the preparation of guidance counselors, it is possible that other programs might be developed in accordance with the design proposed. The administration area might, for example, wish to provide such a master's program. Or the psychology area might wish to develop a measurement-centered clinical master's degree, with a second-year internship consisting of work in the field of testing, or in some phase of research, with perhaps a written report or a thesis as a basis for evaluating the quality of the internship. In fact, any area might, in theory, propose the development of a clinical master's program with the features above proposed, providing "terminal" preparation for some phase of educational practice. It is, however, unlikely that every area will find it reasonable to develop such a program, and we certainly are not recommending that every area do so. (The fate of the Certificate of Advanced Study, as a predoctoral extension of the clinical master's degree, we leave to the clinical areas.)

We are, however, recommending that disciplinary—as distinct from clinical—master's programs be dropped. Providing for no reasonably "terminal" level of preparation for practice, they make little sense to us as natural stages in academic training. For prospective academicians, the emphasis should be on the doctorate alone, for, unlike the disciplinary master's degree, the doctor's degree can be awarded with some understanding of the pattern of training that has gone into its making and an appreciation of the candidate's powers, as evidenced over a period of years, in course work as well as in thesis research.

Our suggestion is, also, to abandon (or to restrict radically) the Ed.M. for General Purposes. Admirable in its flexibility, this degree program has little else to recommend it. It is practically impossible to say what it is supposed to represent, aside from a period of exploration for the student who is not yet sure what further course he wishes to follow. We propose to eliminate awarding a degree for such exploration alone; our aim is to strengthen all the degrees we offer and, in particular, to have all our master's degrees represent basic clinical proficiency in some area of educational practice. For the legitimate purposes of exploratory work, however, we propose that the category "admitted to graduate study only" be reactivated by the School, on a limited basis, as a standard admission category. Such a category would be appropriate for a candidate who wanted the opportunity to take a variety of courses and to test his interests; it would also be suitable for candidates who did not seem clearly admissible to doctoral study as yet, but who seemed to merit a year of trial work. In any event, admission under this category would need to carry the clear advance understanding that no degree was to be granted simply as the result of satisfactory completion of one year's course work. Our long-term efforts should, furthermore, be devoted to informing students at an early stage in their careers of the varied possibilities for educational study and work, so that the need for extended exploration in their graduate years is substantially reduced.

There might still turn out to be special cases—for example, persons with unusual prior experience or training for whom an individually designed master's program seemed both warranted and feasible. Such cases should be considered to fall within the special prerogatives of the Committee on Degrees, rather than in any single area. The Committee on Admissions, in consultation with the Committee on Degrees, might well wish to consider petitions for admission into an individually designed program of the sort mentioned, leading to an Ed.M. for Special Purposes. We are supposing that the candidates for such a degree will be exceedingly few.

The doctor's degree. The degree we are primarily concerned to discuss here is the Doctor of Education degree. But preliminary remarks are necessary concerning the relation of the Ed.D. to the Ph.D. in Education. The former is, at Harvard, under the control of the School, whereas the latter is administered by a joint committee of the Arts and Sciences and Education faculties and is granted under the authority of the Faculty of Arts and Sciences. There is, however, little structural uniformity with respect to these two doctoral labels throughout the country, and the relative quality of the Ed.D. and the Ph.D. in Education does not seem to follow a predictable pattern, although the prestige of the Ph.D. label is almost invariably higher.

The Harvard policy has been to equalize the quality of the two degrees while maintaining their separate structures and recognizing their different potentialities and demands. The structural separateness is built into the University's rules, which limit the permission to grant the Ph.D. to the Faculty of Arts and Sciences alone; the professional schools must develop their own degrees. This separateness is therefore beyond the control of the Graduate School of Education and must be accepted in practice as a given. As in the case of medicine, where the Medical School grants the M.D., and a joint committee with Arts and Sciences administers (for Arts and Sciences) the granting of the Ph.D. in Medical Sciences, so in education we have, analogously, the Ed.D., and the Ph.D. in Education. This structural division has, in our view, little to recommend it, and we favor continued exploration of the possibilities for alternative arrangements. In our ensuing discussion, however, we take such division for granted as a practical current condition of our problem.

The attempt to equalize the quality of the degrees is, however, clearly within the power of our school, and seems to us certainly the correct policy. Moreover, the attempt needs to be constantly made to *improve* the quality of *both*. Aside from matters of program design and requirements, recruitment policy is one key to such improvement. The effort should be made to bring educational careers and advanced educational training to the attention of able students early in their undergraduate period. Various schemes to this effect need to be invented and tried, but at Harvard, there are some easy devices that could be put into effect almost immediately. One is the use of the faculty aide program, which supplies undergraduate research help to our faculty, to interest promising undergraduates in the possibilities of educational research. Another, and potentially much more far-reaching device, is the scheduling of certain of our introductory disciplinary courses at times of the day when they would be accessible to undergraduates. Education, like science, history, and the law, should in fact be made available to Harvard College as part of the general education of its students. No propaganda or special appeals are in point here; the presentation of educational topics in a general and scholarly manner is likely to have a long-term beneficial effect in bringing home to undergraduates the possibilities of educational study and work.

The substantive differentiation of the Ed.D. and Ph.D. in Education is a more difficult problem with which sundry committees have wrestled to small avail for many years. The recurrent suggestion is that the Ed.D. should be the professional or practitioner's degree, and the Ph.D. in Education the academic or scholarly degree. There is much to recommend such a suggestion, but there are also certain problems that it raises. The further differentiation of the Ph.D. in Education from the Ph.D. in the associated departmental discipline needs, for example, to be handled. If the former is to be an academic or scholarly degree, suitable for the application of some discipline to education, how is it to be distinguished from the Ph.D. offered in the department itself where the discipline is cultivated? To suggest that it should draw together *several* disciplines and apply them to education is not only to make it a very difficult degree, both for the student and the committee that administers it; it is not only to make it extremely hard to explain to colleges and universities that might be in a position to hire its graduates; it is also to slant the degree perilously toward the applied side and to intensify the protest of departmental purists against any suggestion that the Ph.D. in Education should represent their particular discipline. On the other hand, it is clear the departments are not prepared themselves to produce the requisite numbers of graduates with an interest in educational applications and a willingness to undertake careers of teaching and scholarship in schools of education; thus the abolition of other channels for such purposes is no real solution.

Suppose, then, that the purists' stand is simply rejected, and that the Ph.D. in Education is especially geared to graduating persons who have a primary identification with, and a solid training in, some scholarly or research discipline, but who also have a genuine focus of interest in educational applications (compare, for instance, the philosopher of education with the philosopher of science or of art). Then could we not further differentiate the Ph.D. in Education, so conceived, from the Ed.D., construed as a professional degree suitable only for the educational practitioner?

Here, we again face an institutional difficulty. The Ed.D. is under the control of the School of Education and commands its resources. The Ph.D. in Education, however, without a department of its own in the Faculty of Arts and Sciences, has no faculty of its own or substantial resources of any other sort. The Committee on the Ph.D. in Education, which administers the degree, is essentially an organizing and governing body, nothing more. It must arrange for students' programs to be properly carried through under the supervision of appropriate advisers. It must negotiate with the several departments, or their faculty representatives, for its students to gain admission to seminars and advanced courses, and for them to receive a share of the departments' limited advising time. This situation sets very real limits to the capacity of the committee to expand and to maneuver. The Ph.D. in Education at Harvard must, in consequence, remain a very limited route to the doctorate, unless its fundamental governing rules are changed.

It seems to us, therefore, that we must hold open the possibility of using the Ed.D. for scholarly training as well as for professional preparation. This is perhaps unfortunate, since it eliminates the clear division between Ed.D. and Ph.D.; yet in view of the difficulties discussed, it seems to us that there is no superior alternative available. We might, however, try to effect a distinction of degree rather than kind, in the following sense: to channel toward the Ph.D. in Education those candidates whose position by virtue of training and interest is closer to the discipline, but whose aim is to develop education as a preferred domain of application, and to channel toward the Ed.D. those whose position is closer to the field of education, but whose aim is to develop the capacity to analyze its problems by certain preferred disciplinary methods. This is not a hard and fast line, to be sure, but it seems to us to indicate a difference of direction that makes sense, and it leaves open the possibility of reinterpretation in the light of future possibilities of expansion and changing demands by students. It also allows for different applications by the several disciplines in accord with variations in the attitudes of their related departments in the Faculty of Arts and Sciences.

The Ed.D., then, is to embrace not only professional and problem-oriented programs, but also scholarly and research programs. We do not, as in the case of the master's degree, propose to suggest a basic design for all Ed.D. programs. The differences in the requirements of the several programs are too great, and the relative demands of specialization loom too large. We trust, moreover, that the several areas will wish to reconsider their own programs and suggest improvements based on their special knowledge and purposes.

Nevertheless, there is one problem to which we wish to address ourselves, and that is the problem of providing for common elements of experience in all the programs for the Ed.D. This is, of course, an aspect of the problem of integration and is the more important at the doctoral level, where the demands of specialization must legitimately take precedence. Somehow, despite such legitimate demands, a significant incorporation of integrating elements must be made, or the basic conception of the study of education in the School will be jeopardized. Indeed, the danger is already evident in the increasing distance and isolation that characterize the several doctoral programs in relation to one another.

The basic conception of the School, as we see it, is one that views the School as a meeting place for significant varieties of scholarship, research, and practice relevant to education. To allow the several doctoral programs to become increasingly separated from one another is thus to threaten this conception in a most fundamental way. Our proposal is to find some method of making common conversations part of the experience of all doctoral students in the School.

We do not favor imposing some substantive core of course work on all programs. Rather, our idea is to capitalize on the increasingly special identities taking shape in students of the different programs, on their growing, but various, methodological skills, on their greater involvements in special problems of research, scholarship, or practice, and on their new enthusiasms for their several fields of study and action. Our notion is to bring all these elements together in critical dialogue centered on the advanced work being done by these students. One significant possibility is a regular colloquium of all doctoral students, attended also by the faculty, where the current work of students, or faculty, could be presented and discussed. Such a colloquium would provide an ideal medium for the confrontation of the different advanced perspectives represented in the School. It would bring students together in a significant way, and might well be capable of fostering a spirit of professional comradeship across programs that does not now exist. It would also bring students together with faculty and provide for both groups an opportunity to educate themselves with respect to the frontier problems of all doctoral fields. Without infringing on the proper development of specialized doctoral training, it would provide an integrating force to counteract the fragmentation that threatens.

There are, unfortunately, various difficulties in working out the concrete organization of such a colloquium. There are, for example, problems of form, of size, of timing, and of responsibility, among others. These problems we have not been able to resolve. We strongly recommend, however, that the matter be taken as a challenge to practical invention and experiment, and that an appropriate agency be designated by the dean to deliberate the issue and prepare a tentative plan for trial in the year after next.

Postdoctoral programs. We recommend the development of postdoctoral programs at the School. With the proposed shift of priorities toward the doctoral level and the increased emphasis on advanced research, scholarship, and professional training, the School could, with relative ease, initiate such program on a moderate scale. There is little question that Harvard University offers rich resources for postdoctoral scholarship and research, and could attract distinguished scholars and outstanding practitioners to such work. There is, furthermore, little doubt that postdoctoral programs would have beneficial effects on the work of the School, on the profession at large, and on the quality of educational inquiries. Education has, in the recent past, suffered from being too narrowly construed as simply a professional subject, and the contrary emphasis on mature research and disinterested scholarship is in itself of high potential merit. Postdoctoral programs could, further, help to develop intellectual and personal links among scholars in diverse fields, all having an interest in the educational relevance of their work. In effect, the School could thus extend its "meeting place" conception over a much wider area than the domain of its own students and alumni.

We do not here wish to make definite and specific proposals as to numbers and types of postdoctoral fellows, or to suggest an admission mechanism or a formal program structure. It seems to us, however, that annual postdoctoral fellowships might be made available, in small numbers, to established researchers, scholars, or professional practitioners who would be invited to spend the year in residence, with no other responsibility than to participate in the scholarly conversations taking place among faculty and students. A further small number of fellowships might also be established for younger scholars or researchers with worthy study projects. There are, in addition, occasional requests by visiting scholars to be attached in some way to the School during the period of their independent visits, to have library privileges, for example, to be introduced to their professional colleagues, or to be allowed to audit certain seminars. Such persons could well be given an honorary research status for the duration of their stay, and would benefit the School by bringing to it their varied backgrounds of experience and thought. We recommend that the initiation of postdoctoral programs be accepted in principle, and that a suitable plan for initial trial be drafted for faculty approval by a committee appointed by the dean.

Nondegree institutes. A professional school cannot, we feel, disregard urgent social needs and problems falling within its purview. Its ultimate goals include the improvement of practice, and it loses in authority if it takes no position on practical issues within its competence. The problem, however, is how a professional school can properly express its position. It cannot easily issue manifestos or engage collectively in public debate. It cannot throw its energies into topical problems without running the risk of distraction from its main concerns with advanced scholarship and training. These concerns need to be protected at all costs, for they are the basis of whatever authority, scholarly or professional, the Graduate School of Education may claim to possess.

The main answer we propose for this problem is the development of short-term nondegree institutes for special purposes of a relatively direct sort. Such special institutes have been tried in the summer school with considerable success. There they have taken the form of short programs directed to special problems of teachers. We are suggesting a systematic and expanded use of such summer institutes, under the authority of the new Committee on Academic Policy of the School, as a service and professional arm of the School.

The institutes might serve a variety of purposes. The dissemination of new ideas on curriculum and methods for teachers in the lower schools, the consideration of problems of college teaching, the provision of brief courses on special problems of city schools, of refresher courses on the computer and new issues raised by educational technology, of philosophical and discussion courses on conflicting educational purposes—all these could well be handled within the institute framework without special intrusion into formal degree programs.

Moreover, the institutes could provide an opportunity for social action of a more direct sort. They could, for example, extend direct help to teachers and administrators of the predominantly Negro schools, colleges, and teacher-training institutions, in curriculum innovation and other educational matters. They could, in short, direct the energies of the School in a concentrated way on social issues falling within the concerns of the educational profession.

Though these institutes could be conducted separately from the degree programs of the School, there would inevitably be an increased demand on faculty energies. Thus we do not recommend a large program. Our idea is for the Academic Policy

Committee to plan for the use of institutes on a long-term and systematic basis, in the light of its considered judgment of the most pressing needs of the moment and the available resources of the School.

The improvement of teaching. Before closing our discussion of programs, we add here certain comments on teaching. We hope that greater attention will be paid to the quality of teaching and advising in our school. It is no secret that the primary Harvard emphasis has by and large been placed on research rather than on teaching, and that the career motivations and academic rewards of the young faculty member are linked more closely to research than to teaching. With our proposed shift in priorities toward doctoral training and the concomitant strengthening of the spirit of research at the School, the quality of our teaching will be ever more in danger of being overlooked for the sake of what are considered more important concerns.

But we believe that the quality of teaching is of major significance, especially in a school of education. True, there is no logical contradiction between the significant advancement of knowledge and the poor teaching of such knowledge, and there is no law that says one must practice what he preaches. There is, however, an anomaly of a pragmatic kind in the neglect of its own teaching practices by an education faculty. Such neglect raises the natural question why professional improvement does not begin at home.

It is, however, not easy to propose a direct attack on this problem. We have been made uncomfortable in the reading of several responses to our alumni questionnaire that complain of poor teaching and poorer advising. What can be done to improve the situation without intruding on the academic freedom of the individual instructor, without prying into his relations with students, without downgrading the genuine importance of research, and without hoping to overthrow the whole reward system of the academic profession?

Indirect and general methods seem to us the most desirable. We have thus introduced the stimulus to experimentation in several courses, proposing such experimentation in the projected Introduction to Education course as well as in the introductory courses offered by the disciplinary areas, courses that are crucial in bringing the disciplines to bear on the general life of the School. We have also stressed the importance of striving for more active forms of teaching in order to elicit the reflective thought, writing, and critical discussion of our students. To this end we have suggested an increased effort to experiment with seminar offerings, tutorials, and individual research courses. We should like here to propose also that senior faculty members take major responsibility for introductory courses, which require both a mature grasp of the subject's technicalities and a relaxed ability to explore its general ramifications. Such courses also provide a natural and continuing challenge to improve the quality of teaching.

With respect to advising, we should encourage each area to explore the special problems of advising within its domain and to work out a reasonable advising quota for its primary affiliates, which would serve as a limitation in the admission of new students to study in the area. And there is much that the areas can do to supplement the formal advisory relationship. They can provide increased opportunity for informal meeting between faculty and students, and they can offer the area faculty a regular opportunity for evaluation of students' performance as well as for early guidance and help in cases of difficulty.

Our earlier suggestion of a common research colloquium for all doctoral students, aside from its hoped-for integrating effect and expected strengthening of professional morale, has a further advantage from the point of view of the doctoral candidate. In current practice, his initial stage is spent in taking courses, often largely within the confines of his program, and, in any case, without formal confrontation by faculty and students of other areas. The qualifying paper, which is, in accordance with current practice, normally written at the end of his course work, is, however, read by a mixed committee of the faculty. For the first time the student finds his work being evaluated from quite unfamiliar perspectives within the School. The experience often comes as a rude awakening for both student and faculty members concerned. The projected common research colloquium would have the advantage of introducing the doctoral student immediately to all the areas in the School in the context of research discussion, where differing intellectual standards and diverse methodologies would be made manifest. This sort of early orientation would also, we feel, be likely to supplement the process of formal advising.

Concurrently with his growth in general sophistication, however, the student should be achieving his specialized professional identity through his work in his area. Here, beyond formal courses, the student might well be incorporated into area life, both intellectual and social. He could, for example, no doubt contribute to as well as profit from certain of the area's regular scholarly discussions, and his increased social contact with the faculty would in itself be beneficial in overcoming what is often felt as genuine isolation.

Moreover, we believe that our students have much to tell us about the programs and requirements that are so much a part of their lives at Harvard. There is a precedent at our school of employing our own graduate students for temporary periods on our administrative staffs with, by and large, brilliant success. Could we not incorporate more of their dedication, acuteness, sincerity, and sound judgment into the life of the School by talking with them more about the programs under which they are studying and the procedures and requirements they are trying to meet? Could we not involve them profitably in discussions of area problems, operations, planning, and even academic standards and evaluation? We recommend this idea, at any rate, to the several areas for their deliberation.

We should like also to recommend that the School establish

special counseling services for students. We train counselors, we know the value of counseling, and yet we do not have adequate provision for the counseling of our own students. Such provision would, we feel, also help to raise student morale and to improve, without intruding upon, the relations between students and faculty.

RESEARCH

The problems surrounding the organization of research at the School are among the most complex that we have considered. After listing some of the major factors that seem to us relevant, we shall specify these problems and make our proposals regarding what should be done.

The first factor to note is the special character of research in a school of education. Such research is linked, fairly directly, to public policy and to professional practice. Our programs of research lead into public life and are rightly judged by the public as the School's responsible contribution to that life. Second, the demands on schools of education for educational research and development are already enormous, and are likely to increase within the foreseeable future. The pressures on individual faculty members to engage in research-related activities of a variety of sorts for universities, schools, private and government agencies, and professional groups are also very great and are likely to continue to grow. Third, the senior professorship at Harvard is so conceived as to preclude purely research activity without teaching; it grants freedom to the individual professor to choose his research commitments and develop them as he sees fit, but it requires of every professor that he in fact be a teacher. And the Harvard professorship cannot be supported by research grants, but must be supported exclusively by endowment funds.

These factors create a number of practical difficulties. There is the perennial problem, for each individual professor, of creating for himself a proper balance between teaching activities on the one hand and research and professional activities on the other. Given the enormous demands of the latter, and his perfectly legitimate desire to respond to such demands, he is drawn into ever-increasing involvement, to the detriment of his teaching, not to mention his leisure time and his health. Even when his teaching does not suffer, it becomes more and more oriented toward his special research interests, and less and less concentrated on those introductory and general courses through which he speaks to the student body at large. We have already suggested how important it is for the senior faculty member to take responsibility for general and introductory courses, where his technical grasp and maturity give him special strength.

Nor can the answer be simply to restrict the senior professor's research involvements and tie him more closely to teaching. For one thing, such a restriction seems to run counter to his assumed freedom to follow his research interests wherever they may lead, and would in any case be difficult to formulate and to apply. Second, the professor makes a genuine and important contribution through his research, and it is not clear how much of such a potential contribution ought to be sacrificed to the interests of teaching, even if an applicable formula were available. Finally, the School's major research programs themselves require that senior faculty members' energies be devoted to them in order to provide continuity and stability to the School's research policy and long-term output.

In fact, a fundamental problem for the School itself, rather than for the individual professor, is how to cope with the growing demands upon it for engagement in research and development projects—without evasion, but at the same time without following a course of easy and irresponsible involvement. A course to be avoided above all is the initial commitment of the School to a project that then loses the attention of senior members and is turned over to junior staff to be carried through in fragmented fashion, and without adequate evaluation, until assigned funds are expended. Clearly a long-term policy for the

School's selection of major research projects is needed. Clearly, also, the active and continuous participation of senior faculty members in the management of such research is needed if it is to be executed in a responsible manner.

Such needs, however, draw heavily upon the energies of senior faculty members, and also draw them away from a concern with teaching. Furthermore, the professor cannot, by the terms of his Harvard employment, be wholly withdrawn from teaching even were such withdrawal otherwise desirable, nor, as noted above, can his salary be financed out of short-term research grants.

We have, then, a fundamental dilemma that is quite independent of the individual balance a professor strikes between his teaching and his research: in order to guarantee a stable and responsible execution of research policy by the School, the senior professor must be increasingly committed to research development and management; in order to guarantee a high quality of teaching and to fulfill the conditions of his employment, he cannot be so committed. To withdraw from major research commitments altogether is an impossible course for the School; on the other hand, to accept them responsibly, while maintaining the traditional expectations of the professor, seems equally impossible.

To deal with these issues, we propose a revised conception of faculty obligations, as well as certain guiding principles for the School's research commitments. Turning first to the question of faculty obligations, we propose, to begin with, that purely external demands on a professor's time be limited by the University's rule that restricts his absence from Cambridge to an average of one day a week. Priority must, in other words, clearly be given to University work, performed in residence. At the same time, however, there needs to be a revision of formal teaching loads. Earlier practice at the School was for the faculty member to teach five half courses a year, and, in more recent years, to teach four half courses, as a full load. Such a definition of a full load makes it, in our opinion, almost mathematically impossible for the professor to perform excellently in teaching, do a proper job in advising doctoral candidates, and also share in managing the major research projects to which the School is committed. Our suggestion is to recognize that the formal teaching of courses is only one sort of teaching that goes on in an advanced school; the teaching that takes place informally through advising, as well as through the informal guidance of apprentices on research projects, needs also to be counted as part of the teaching engaged in by a professor. Given such recognition, we suggest that the formal teaching load be set at two half courses, plus an optional advanced seminar. It should be strongly emphasized, however, that no reduction is here contemplated of the total teaching time of the professor; what is in question is simply a revised understanding of the sorts of teaching in which a professor is normally engaged. The reduction in formal course load is therefore definitely not intended to imply a diminished commitment to teaching. Such a reduction would result in fewer formal courses, but, we hope, better-taught courses. Moreover, we have already suggested that the number of advisees assigned to each faculty member, particularly doctoral advisees, be strictly limited by each area in accord with an area quota reflected in admission policy.

To provide balance in the professor's formal teaching, however, we suggest that the recommended load reduction be supplemented by a principle of variety based on a threefold distinction among formal courses. There are, for example, general or introductory courses, which are addressed to all students, and which initiate them into the special subject. Then there are intermediate systematic courses, addressed primarily to students within a certain program, or field, of specialization. Finally, there are research seminar courses, addressed primarily to mature students capable of working on "frontier" problems that engage the professor himself. Our recommendation is that a faculty member, in particular a senior professor, should normally teach courses of all three types. He might, for example, offer one general course, one systematic course, and one research seminar in a single year. Or he might teach all three types over a period of two (or perhaps even three) years.

In any event, he ought not to withdraw wholly into his own research sphere, but speak regularly to students outside his specialty. Conversely, of course, he ought not only to teach introductory courses, but he should offer advanced courses and seminars as well, in order to train students in the methods of research and scholarship and help prepare them for creative work. In consequence, the recommended reduction in formal course load ought not to result in isolating the professor either from advanced students in his field or from the general class of students within the School. The saving in time allowed by the reduced formal load might, furthermore, then be applied (in part at least) to the informal teaching and guidance of graduate student apprentices in projects of the School. Such application would allow a greater investment of the senior faculty's effort in such undertakings without contradiction of the teaching function or violation of the conditions of the professorship.

We turn now to the question of the School's research projects. We have already stressed the importance of a selection policy as well as the necessity of putting the support of the senior faculty behind selected projects. We are here concerned not with a faculty member's own research, either nonsponsored or supported by a grant to him as an individual. Rather, what concerns us are major projects that tend to commit us as a school. Here we have, in effect, "shop-creating" grants, where funds are awarded to the School through the dean, who is required to manage the operation. Examples at Harvard in recent years are SUPRAD (School and University Program for Research and Development); the sponsorship of a comprehensive high school in Aiyetoro, Western Nigeria; Project Physics, a nationwide project to develop a humanistically and historically oriented physics course for high school students; and the Research and Development Center, established through support of the United States

Office of Education. Such large projects cannot be acquired by the School merely as ancillary activities that can be run by junior executives and exist simply as side issues for the senior faculty. Our proposed reduction of formal teaching loads and our incorporation of research guidance into the teaching function are intended to allow for increased participation on the part of the senior faculty both in the selection and in the management of major projects.

As for a policy of selection, we hope that the new Committee on Research and Development will provide the continuous and deliberate attention to research proposals that will help in developing the outlines of a policy. Further, the dean will normally have available for preliminary review the counsel provided by the representatives of the six areas as well as the senior faculty itself, and he will no doubt also wish to bring major issues of selection to the whole faculty for study and debate. Only through such processes of deliberation by faculty groups concerned with specific proposals can concrete policy grow.

Nevertheless we should like here to recommend certain guiding principles. First, there should be thorough study and discussion of all major proposals, in accordance with a procedure of review to be decided by the dean. Second, the management of all major projects must rest with the senior faculty, and at least one senior member must be engaged in the management of each such project. Third, no major proposal should be accepted without appropriate advance commitments by senior faculty members that guarantee their active support of the project until the time of its termination. Fourth, no major project should be undertaken unless it is linked in specifiable, though perhaps indirect, ways with the advanced training functions of the School; for instance, our graduate students might carry out supervised research for such a project. This last principle seems to us desirable in that it ties the research-management function of senior faculty members to their teaching function, in line with the expanded concept of teaching earlier suggested. This principle seems to us further desirable in providing another form of integration for the School, preventing projects from becoming merely externally attached to the School's activities, and ensuring their continuous connection with advanced training.

NEEDS AND DEVELOPMENT OF AREAS

In the present section, we present certain ideas concerning the current needs and future development of the six areas of the School. No doubt the areas will themselves wish to determine their needs and plan their development, but they may appreciate having our suggestions as a springboard for their own analyses and deliberations. It should be stressed that the ideas we now offer are intended as suggestions rather than firm recommendations.

Humanities. We currently have history and philosophy represented, but we no longer have a program in comparative education as such, having given up the conception of comparative education as an independent subject and adopted the notion that comparative studies should rather be integrated into regional or area studies. We suggest that the latter approach could probably best be carried out in the context of the Center for Studies in Education and Development. The Center has, since its inception, been perhaps closest to the domains of economics and government, but it has engaged in numerous field studies in other lands, and it has been characterized by an attempt to set the technical problems of educational planning within a general humanistic framework. It seems to us both feasible and desirable to expand the outlook of the Center somewhat, so that it may also foster studies of a comparative kind, within the larger context of its present operations.

We also suggest that the present scope of history and philosophy offerings be expanded. Our history offerings are now limited primarily to the history of American education; we should strive to present a wider view of the subject. Similarly, our philosophy offerings are largely systematic and contemporary in focus; our long-range goal should be to develop the history of educational philosophy in depth. In sum, we are suggesting an expansion of the comparative and historical dimensions of humanistic studies.

Social sciences. Our only senior member in this area is a sociologist, and we have no Ed.D. program in any other social science. Ideally, we should develop also the fields of economics, political science, and anthropology so that we can train doctoral students in these subjects, with emphasis on educational applications. For the present we suggest that an expansion in the number of doctoral students in sociology of education be contemplated, for we have the capacity, with present faculty resources, to absorb such expansion. We hope, in short, that this area will undergo considerable growth in the coming years.

Psychology. The dominant need here seems to be coordination of our resources and programs. We currently offer a doctoral program based in the Laboratory for Research in Instruction, another based in the Laboratory of Human Development, and psychologically oriented programs in the guidance area. A faculty committee of the School is currently preparing a report on programs in educational psychology, and this report should help to coordinate our efforts in this area. We wish, in general, to suggest that the common elements of all our programs of advanced training in psychology be made more salient, and that an attempt be made to increase the communication among the diverse specializations represented. The School is strongly staffed in psychology; what is mainly required now is greater focus.

Administration. Here we find an asymmetrical state of development. The Administrative Career Program, which trains people to be school superintendents, has had a considerable degree of success, so far as we can judge by responses of people in the field. On the other hand, there are two needs that have been repeatedly pointed out to us by our own staff, by alumni, and by our outside consultants. One is the need to develop the field of administrative theory and research, and to strengthen the thesis program in administration. The other is the need to provide programs of training for school principalship.

As to the first, we do indeed suggest that administrative theory and research be developed, jointly with the social sciences and humanities areas, and that the thesis program for the doctorate in administration be strengthened. With respect to the school principalship, our suggestion is that a program be developed by the teaching area, for such a program requires close contact with issues of method, curriculum, and supervision, and should overlap considerably with programs centering on these matters. The teaching area may well wish to call upon the administration area for its advice and collaboration in developing a suitable program.

Teaching. In addition to the suggested program for the training of principals, we need to develop the areas of curriculum and supervision as foci of advanced study and training. Our suggestion is, however, to keep such study and training tied, for the most part, to the specific problems confronting the teaching of a given subject. General treatments of curriculum and supervision should certainly not be ruled out, but they should be encouraged to grow out of more specific preoccupations.

With respect to the resources of the School for handling such specific preoccupations, we have many gaps, to be sure, and they have been repeatedly pointed out to us by alumni, staff, and consultants having special interests in certain subjects. We do not presently have special staff or doctoral programs for the teaching of art, music, classics, foreign languages, or English as a second language, nor do we have staff or programs dealing with adult education, business education, audiovisual education, vocational education, preschool education, higher education, physical education, or special education.

Lack of special staff or programs does not necessarily imply lack of interest in such topics. We should, indeed, be prepared to encourage suitable doctoral students to deal with these within the limits of our present resources, and we should be willing to design individual programs for such students, making use, where possible, of relevant resources elsewhere in the University. Further, we might attempt to move toward a limited expansion in a very few selected fields; development of projects in such fields might be followed by eventual staffing, depending upon a future assessment by the faculty.

It is clear, however, that the fact that we lack staff and programs in certain areas does not in itself prove a need for expansion in those areas. Further, it is clear that it would be extremely unwise for us to expand, in programs or staff, in all the missing fields noted above, for we should then have a series of weak one-man operations or "shops," necessarily lacking in power and depth, and, to a greater or lesser degree, out of touch with the major resources of the School. A wiser course is to improve current operations and to capitalize upon the substantial strengths of the School in certain fields in such a way as to consolidate and advance our programs within these fields. In the field of language, for example, we currently have three senior professors, and so an expansion of language-related programs clearly makes sense. In sum, we recommend consolidation and expansion based upon current School and University resources, tailoring of individual programs for selected students in fields lacking formal programs, and moving toward a very limited expansion in selected new fields of teaching over the coming years.

The question of an experimental school or clinical facility for training and supervision of teachers, as well as for curriculum development, is one that poses various difficulties. Clearly some facility of this sort is an absolute necessity for the study and training programs of the School. One possibility is to design and operate an experimental school of our own. Such a school, however, runs the risk of developing a selected student population and an unhealthy ingroup atmosphere; it is likely to be excessively subject to alumni and faculty pressures. Another possibility is to gain the privilege of working within schools, public or private, that are not operated by us. The difficulty here is that control is exercised by school officials, and that, as guests, our capacities for experimentation are severely limited.

We are inclined to favor still a third course: that we strive to enter into relations with school systems not under our control, whereby we may be granted "functional control" of conditions of learning within selected schools. Such relations would give us free access to certain schools and would provide a natural setting for critical experimentation with curriculum, methods, and training operations. Relations of this sort require, however, that we be prepared to work with the school systems in question in a cooperative and reciprocal manner. We need to be ready to provide leadership and initiative and a degree of practical help. Moreover, we need to find able school people and to assist them in developing their competences; we should, for example, be prepared to appoint them to our own staff, on a part-time basis, for extended periods. (And married women graduates of our school might be employed as part-time teaching replacements for such people in the schools; this is one answer to the wish of many such graduates to return to educational careers.) Such relations between school systems and the Harvard Graduate School of Education would need to be carefully and patiently developed; but they would provide a satisfactory arrangement, in our opinion, for clinical training and experimentation in a live school setting. In general, we should explore and develop such relations for the purposes of clinical training, with a variety of educational agencies, and we should be prepared to maintain joint appointments with them in support of such efforts. At the same time, we need to expand and diversify our total clinical potential, designing special classroom settings where limited innovations may be initially tried with students, arranging situations for trying out pretested ideas in more conventional circumstances, and planning teacher-training facilities of various kinds.

Guidance. As in the case of the psychology area, the need seems to be greater coordination of efforts and programs. Such coordination presents special problems because the field itself is characterized by a variety of specializations, and there seems to be little agreement on conception and practice with respect to training for such specializations. The careers available to graduates in this area are also extremely varied, and the field is itself in a state of transition and growth. (We shall try to frame our discussion in terms of concepts and divisions currently familiar in the practice of the Harvard Graduate School of Education.)

At Harvard, the situation may be characterized as follows: we offer a master's program for guidance counselors and Ed.D. programs in the administration of guidance services, school psychology, counseling psychology, and research in careers. The master's program for guidance counselors should, in our opinion, be reworked to conform to the general "one year plus" design already recommended for all clinical master's programs in the School. The graduate of such a master's program is normally employed in a secondary school, and his work typically requires him to carry out program and college advising as well as testing, vocational guidance, and referral for therapy to appropriate agencies. His task is many-sided and not as heavily imbued with elements of psychology as are those of counseling psychologist and school psychologist.

The professions of school psychology and counseling psychology are more closely linked, through the language, literature, and conceptual apparatus of psychology, though they are characterized by other differences; for school psychology is concerned with small children and is diagnostic, remedial, and psychoanalytic in its general orientation, whereas counseling is concerned with adolescents and young adults, and is oriented more toward nonremedial and nondirective or "ego-identity" approaches. We suggest that there should be substantial overlapping in the doctoral training of school psychologists and counseling psychologists, with specialization at a late stage. Such overlapping would contribute to the integration of the School's work and would be, in our opinion, beneficial to both of these specialties. Further coordination with the present human development program might also be seriously considered.

A smaller but still considerable overlapping of the guidance administration program with that of school psychology and counseling seems to us reasonable, with perhaps an added link to the administration area. The research program seems amenable to similar treatment. Its scope might well be expanded to include a variety of problems having to do with counseling, guidance, and school psychology, rather than being restricted to research in careers. It should then overlap considerably with the school psychology and counseling programs, but should embrace specialized research training, perhaps forming special ties with the two laboratories attached to the School: the Laboratory of Human Development, and the Laboratory for Research in Instruction.

The picture that emerges reveals, first, a single high-quality master's program for guidance counselors, and second, a single core providing substantial unity to all doctoral programs in the area, that is, in school psychology, counseling psychology, administration, and research. These various doctoral programs would all be differentiated in the later stages of training, the administration and the research programs forming their own special ties to relevant external agencies.

Assuming such a picture, we are clearly understaffed in this area. Aside from individual staff needs, there is also a need for stronger ties with clinical psychology and the profession of psychiatry. We suggest that the possibilities be explored of forging new associations with the Harvard Psychiatric Services and with faculty members of the Medical School, the School of Public

Health, and the Department of Social Relations. It goes without saying that increased and improved opportunities must also be made available for supervised clinical practice in appropriate agencies of widely varied sorts, for such practice is the heart of training in all the clinical areas.

CONCLUSION

Having now presented our recommendations and the considerations underlying them, it remains for us here to issue certain cautionary statements as to how they should be regarded and to draw some general conclusions. First, it is clear that there are many issues that we have not resolved. We have settled neither the most abstract and general questions of philosophy nor the most detailed and specific questions of operational procedure. Our intent has been to deal rather with those problems of policy that reflect guiding conceptions of educational study and are therefore of controlling significance. We can hardly, however, hope to have provided an exhaustive treatment even of such policy issues. Many related questions will need to be raised and resolved by the several areas, as well as by appropriate committees of the faculty. We hope, nevertheless, to have provided significant directions for the future development of the Harvard Graduate School of Education, as well as useful statements of underlying issues that may help to crystallize general discussion and analysis of the graduate study of education. It remains for others to judge whether we have succeeded.

The emphasis on future discussion and analysis is not a mere rhetorical device. Anyone who deals with practical issues as complex as those that have occupied us must realize how easy it is to go astray, and must welcome the test and correction of future experience and criticism. Thus we propose not a dogmatic utopia, but a fallible set of hypotheses; though they seem to us warranted, they require critical scrutiny especially if, and as, they are carried into practice. Our structural proposals arise, indeed, from our wish to create conditions that will favor continuing critical discussion not only regarding School policy, but regarding the substantive problems and methods germane to the study of education.

Our recommendations are, in one special sense, utopian. We have not much concerned ourselves with costs. Clearly, improvement in education, as elsewhere, requires funds. The proposals we have made for increased staffing in certain of the areas, for improved and expanded relations with school systems and clinical facilities, for improved supervisory arrangements, for a reduction of master's level commitments concurrent with an extension to a "one year plus" design—all presuppose considerable financial support. They also presuppose a relatively peaceful world. Granted such a world, our proposals may be taken to indicate the sorts of reform that we believe merit support as contributing to the improvement of the graduate study of education.

Such improvement depends, basically, upon breaking down the narrow and isolating conceptions that confine education on all sides. Education is not simply an affair of the classroom, nor is the study of education merely a professional subject required of prospective teachers. Education is better conceived broadly as an organizing perspective from which all problems of culture and learning may be viewed. To place the issues of professional practice within such a context is to relate it to the whole life of the university. The special task of a university school of education is to facilitate such relationship, and in so doing to benefit both practice and scholarship.

This task is an exceedingly demanding one, for it requires a school of education to assimilate diversity and to live with the resulting tension. Without the protection of the departmental walls which shield the disciplines at the university's center, situated rather at the periphery in contact with the external world, the professional school must mediate between the diversified knowledge available within and the pressures of practice impinging from without. It must be marvelously integrated in order to survive, let alone prosper. The integration of a school of education is especially urgent just because of the breadth of its concerns. Ever present is the temptation to be satisfied with an immature integration, resting on a simple blindness to complexity, an overconfidence in some static synthesis of facts and doctrine, or a weak faith in an autonomous theoretical discipline as yet unborn. We have urged resistance to such temptation, proposing as our fundamental integrating principle the institution of continuing discussions among all those who have something to contribute to advancing the study of education or improving the educational art.

It is through such discussion, in the scholarly setting of the University, that the Graduate School of Education may hope to engender the intellectual excitement and the critical climate in which new ideas are born, and through which able students may receive their proper training. The provision of an intellectual and critical environment of this sort underlies the university's claim to leadership. Such an environment cannot be manufactured on order, nor can it be quickly grown. It requires patient nurture, a long-range view, and a faith in the power of ideas. If our school is to strive for educational leadership, it must set itself to cultivate such an environment.

APPENDIXES

APPENDIX A

A HISTORICAL PERSPECTIVE
Arthur G. Powell

A UNITY OF PURPOSE

Charles Francis Adams, Jr., had had enough. The distinguished industrialist and Harvard Overseer thought the indirect efforts of President Charles W. Eliot to reform American schools were hardly sufficient to the task. The only effective way to influence the schools, Adams told Eliot in 1893, was to take them over and run them from Cambridge! Adams' frustration arose from his disappointment with the results of Harvard College admission examinations. But it was part of a larger concern for the schools felt by many Harvardians in the 1890's. Eliot shared much of Adams' complaint, but shunned his extreme remedy. He thought indirect efforts, if pursued on enough fronts, could produce the desired results.

The establishment of courses in education at Harvard in 1891 was part of Eliot's effort to exert effective influence on the schools. His purposes were often expressed in terms of the national interest but, like most of what he did, they were also fundamentally concerned with the advancement of Harvard. At this time Eliot feared that his monumental effort to establish professional education in law and medicine on the base of the bachelor's degree might fail because of the very long time it took students to complete their training.

One solution was to shorten the college course. Another was to lower the age of college freshmen. Eliot tried both solutions, but both depended on the ability of the lower schools to accomplish more in a shorter period of time. Eliot had many definite ideas about how this could be done, and tried in a number of ways to disseminate them and put them into effect. Perhaps the Report of the Committee of Ten was his most famous, but no less significant in the long run was his decision, after local agitation had opened the question, to offer education courses.

Thus at the beginning the study of education served the interests of the University. The coming of Assistant Professor Paul H. Hanus was expected to advance Harvard's influence over the schools in several ways. Hanus administered a series of short special-methods courses for teachers or prospective teachers taught by regular Harvard professors. These augmented traditional techniques of influence such as admission examinations, syllabuses, and school texts written by Harvard professors. Hanus traveled about to establish better relations with public schools. He assisted other Eliot enterprises, notably the Schools Examination Board, which supplied a team of Harvard professors to examine a school at its request and expense. Finally, Hanus gave courses on school organization and theory.

Hanus proved an excellent choice for Eliot's purposes. He used his classroom and pen to advocate what were basically Eliot's ideas. Among these were the adoption by schools of the new subjects that American universities had developed since the Civil War: English literature, science, and history; the adoption of methods of teaching, such as laboratory science, which stressed the use of the senses over rote memorization; and the adoption of the elective system by secondary schools.

What is significant here is not the particular content of Hanus' teaching, but that it conformed so well to the general interest of the University as defined by the president. Some faculty members did attack Hanus' courses for tending toward the speculative theories of mind taught in normal schools. And Hanus' blunt and undiplomatic temperament often made his position more precarious than it had to be. But he was not spinning speculative theories or dealing with narrow problems of method, and Eliot knew this full well. Eliot had always disliked normal-school pedagogy, but respected what Hanus was doing, and often said that he hoped a class of "professional educationists" might be trained at Harvard to give leadership to American education. In 1901 he gave Hanus tenure; in 1906 the courses in education were removed from the Division of Philosophy and made into a separate division.

SOURCES OF SEPARATION

Near the end of the first decade of this century, the bonds of interest between the Division of Education and the University began to weaken. Hanus, understandably, sought to hold them together in order to get support and money. Thus he argued, beyond the time when such argument was convincing, that Harvard-trained teachers would recruit high school boys for Harvard College, and that there was great danger that the influence of Teachers College would cause students to gather in New York, not Cambridge.

But times had changed. The University administration was no longer worried about the possibilities of decreasing enrollment or of losing contact with high schools. The professional schools and the College were thriving. The uncertainties that had motivated Eliot's actions in the nineties no longer existed. Harvard was stable, and its new president, A. Lawrence Lowell, was more inclined to look inward at the procedures by which liberal education was carried on. Finally, the appointment policy of the Faculty of Arts and Sciences now emphasized productive scholarship to the extent that few men outside the Division of Education had a direct or professional interest in teaching or the schools. Many of the professors who had supported Hanus in the nineties were dead. Those who remained, such as Albert Bushnell Hart of the Department of History, were under increasing criticism from their own colleagues for being unscholarly.

At the same time that the Division of Education became less relevant as a political agency of the University, Hanus' interests shifted away from a preoccupation with academic curriculum reform. Hanus was, it should be kept in mind, one of the first generation of university professors of education. He had to build up the reputation of his subject and calling, which at Harvard meant separating himself from the normal-school tradition.

His growing sense of the special character of education as a body of knowledge manifested itself in two general ways. First, he sought a method of procedure that would produce valid, unassailable conclusions; always an empiricist by temperament, he became an advocate of scientific induction as the chief method of solving educational problems. Second, the kind of educational problem that he thought important changed significantly. Increasingly he became preoccupied with the large numbers of city children who stayed in school even though they were not planning to attend college. By 1910 he was a leader in the Massachusetts movement for separate vocational schools. Hanus' advocacy of science and induction placed him clearly in the mainstream of Harvard thinking; but his growing interest in vocational and other nonacademic kinds of education did not interest President Lowell or other high officials.

After 1912 the interests of the Division of Education diverged more sharply from those of the University. The faculty had not grown very much in numbers during its first twenty years. Hanus labored alone until certain Cambridge ladies provided money in 1897 for an additional teacher to repeat courses at Radcliffe. Later, Mr. and Mrs. Joseph Lee of Boston supported a young instructor named Henry Wyman Holmes in order to advance the ideas of Friedrich Froebel. In 1911 Lowell persuaded his friend John Moors to take an active role as head of the Overseers' Committee to Visit the Division of Education, removed Hanus from the Division chairmanship, and replaced him with Holmes.

Several prominent Boston and New York businessmen joined this committee and became interested in the work of the Division. Men such as Lincoln Filene, James J. Storrow, Joseph Lee, Felix Warburg, and Jerome Greene all viewed the work of the Division in terms of the problems of urban America. They saw little connection between the Division and the schools attended by their own children. Hence they did not see the Division as serving the interest of Harvard College. But they did see the desperate need to deal somehow with the masses of urban young people. For Joseph Lee, the problem was to restore in urban America the older rural values of play and recreation. For Lincoln Filene, the problem was to provide vocational advice for youngsters. For Felix Warburg, the problem was to offer vocational education for those not bound for college. And so it went.

Those men were persuaded to give money for appointments in several new fields of educational activity such as play and vocational guidance, which shaped much of the Division's work for the next generation. Perhaps the most revealing appointment was in secondary education. The problem here was no longer seen to be training teachers through special-methods courses taught by regular Harvard academic professors. Assistant Professor Alexander Inglis, appointed in 1914, was concerned with broadening the content and philosophy of secondary education to meet what he believed to be the needs of the new masses of students. Inglis' conception of secondary education conformed perfectly with the new fields of activity represented in the Division.

From 1913 to 1917 the number of faculty, graduate and undergraduate students, and courses in the Division all doubled. The new subjects were genuinely new; they did not evolve from prior academic offerings. The professors were largely men who had in their earlier careers created in the schools the subjects that they later taught at Harvard. George E. Johnson, for example, had established supervised playgrounds in Pittsburgh. Frederick G. Nichols, appointed in 1922, had pioneered in commercial education in Rochester.

These men and others had been radical innovators whose purpose at Harvard was to promote through teaching, writing, and other activity what they had done in the schools. Their presence gave the Division of Education a sense of uniqueness and purpose that Henry Holmes took pride in. They were evidence for his contention that the profession had special careers that demanded special training. But they accentuated the diverging purposes of the Division and the Faculty of Arts and Sciences.

The new courses were clearly vocational in purpose. They trained people for specific jobs. President Eliot had not opposed vocationalism in undergraduate courses. President Lowell, however, wanted to protect liberal education, and disliked the growing vocational orientation of the Division. He therefore supported the request of Holmes and Hanus to convert the Division into a separate professional school. The educationists wanted freedom from the Faculty of Arts and Sciences to expand their program; Lowell wanted the Faculty of Arts and Sciences free from the vocationalism of the Division. After a long search for funds, Hanus obtained a grant from the General Education Board, a leading foundation, to start the endowment, and the University gave and raised the rest.

AUTONOMY AND CONFLICT

The creation of the Graduate School of Education in 1920 was an event of great importance. The Division of Education now became a separate faculty, acquired an endowment, controlled its own, new degrees, and admitted women to degree candidacy at Harvard for the first time. But the establishment of the School did not represent any change of purpose. The greater resources now available enabled its faculty to do more effectively what it had already set out to do: in the main, to offer specific and practical training for particular educational jobs. The expansion of the curriculum and the attempt to attract as many students as possible were consistent with this purpose. The profession seemed to demand that this kind of training be extended as widely as possible. Henry Holmes, who became the first dean of the School, believed Harvard could do no less than meet this demand.

The School's existence gave new visibility to Harvard's undertaking in education. As one of the University's esteemed professional schools, it became subject to new demands and comparisons that had never had to be made before. President Lowell immediately took a large role in actively directing its fortunes. Lowell saw the School as an example of the historical shift in the character of professional training: where practitioners were once prepared by apprenticeship in narrow techniques of procedure, they were now prepared in special schools that taught general principles. What Lowell thought important was not the institutional change but the switch from narrow techniques to general principles. This accounted, he believed, for the spectacular rise of the Harvard Law School and for the growing eminence of the Business School.

The problem of the profession of education was that it lacked general principles. The primary task of the Graduate School of Education in its early years, Lowell thought, was to hire men who would find those principles. He felt that the study of statistics provided the best opportunity to develop educational principles. Data were already available to be analyzed, especially in the voluminous records of Harvard College. Lowell himself had dabbled in such analysis, and, at his request, so had Holmes.

In 1920 Lowell rejected all of the major appointments proposed by Holmes for the new school's faculty on the grounds that the suggested individuals possessed mere technical competence and insufficient scholarly power. Holmes realized that Lowell's objection challenged the very purposes of the Graduate School of Education. He retorted that the men he wanted were by no means unscholarly; indeed their books were highly praised and very influential. They were not directly concerned with general principles, it was true, but with the practical problems of particular educational jobs. That kind of specificity, said Holmes, was what students in a professional school such as the Graduate School of Education wanted and needed. They would hardly resort to the School at all unless their vocational needs were met. He pointedly mentioned that the earlier reputation of the Division of Education within the profession had depended far less on its psychologist than on its man in secondary education.

Thus the School opened its doors on a note of doubt and disagreement. Holmes was uncertain whether it could draw students. The salaries of teachers were low following World War I; there were no Massachusetts state requirements to force teachers to attend; the new degrees might not catch on. But students did attend, and in increasing numbers. By 1926 there were 529 in the School, 448 of whom were candidates for degrees. Eighty-three were full-time students. A well-publicized study of schools of education ranked Harvard's as third best in the country in 1925. The School's success seemed assured.

Yet the conflict between Holmes and Lowell intensified. Lowell wanted the Graduate School of Education to fit the pattern of other Harvard professional schools. That pattern emphasized a lengthy training period in general principles for young and inexperienced full-time students who would never need to attend school again. The School of Education had none of these characteristics. Its students were primarily experienced teachers who attended part-time in order to gain practical knowledge for advancement in the profession.

Lowell realized that the immediate needs of these students impeded the development of a curriculum based on general principles. The Education Faculty, on the other hand, saw the students as those mature, aspiring professionals who most appreciated and profited from its instruction. Holmes, deeply troubled by conflicting pressures, defended both the curriculum and the student body, but the latter with decreasing conviction.

Early in 1924 Lowell suggested that the School develop a special curriculum for full-time inexperienced candidates. This proposal forced a lengthy and elaborate effort to reassess the purposes and procedures of the School that lasted for the next seven years. Many changes were made, including the conversion of the master of education degree to a two-year degree in 1927. Holmes had come to agree with Lowell that the School should be adjusted, in ways mainly affecting the student body, to conform to the pattern of other Harvard professional schools. By 1931 Holmes thought that an adequate adjustment had been made, and the way opened to a new era in the history of the profession of education.

THE PROFESSIONAL IDEAL MATURES

The large number of reports, discussions, and new procedures produced between 1924 and 1931 can best be seen as an effort to preserve the purposes established at Harvard a decade earlier within a pattern of professional training analogous to that of its other professional schools. The principal goal was still to train students for particular educational jobs by faculty members who had participated in the establishment and development of those jobs. What changed was the conception of timing and sequence of that preparation.

Between 1924 and 1931 the focus of debate and discussion within the faculty switched from external interest in fields of activity and service to an internal concern for the problems of professionalism in education. Thus the master of education degree was emphasized over the doctorate as a professional degree. The student body was expected to consist eventually of full-time inexperienced students. The "raw A.B." would be given relatively final professional training for all forms of professional service during his two years of study.

The School attempted to guarantee the quality of its graduates by developing new ways to measure their professional competence. The passing of courses no longer guaranteed a degree. Students had to fulfill an apprenticeship requirement and pass two written examinations. Holmes hoped that the School would be able to create examinations to measure all important kinds of competence, including "professional judgment," and dispense with course credits altogether. The full implications of professionalism were never carried out. They would have included the elimination of women as candidates for Harvard degrees, though women would still have attended the School by way of Radcliffe, and the creation of a separate campus, similar to that of the Business School, where a professional *esprit de corps* would be formed in an atmosphere of common association and camaraderie.

Doubtless this effort to make the School of Education procedurally consistent with other Harvard professional schools met some of Lowell's objections, but professionalism came to have additional and more controversial meanings in the early thirties. Holmes and Francis T. Spaulding, his protégé and eventual successor, elaborated an ideology of the curriculum widely divergent from Lowell's notions of the proper content of professional study.

"The professional ideal" required that the curriculum be suffused with a utilitarian orientation toward the field and the educational jobs to be done. It rejected the academic ideals found not only in the Faculty of Arts and Sciences but among those faculties of education elsewhere, notably at the University of Chicago, that emphasized the study of education as a scholarly subject and the development of general scientific principles. The professional ideal thus confirmed and intensified the School's orientation toward practicality, job training, and the field. One of the School's most brilliant students was dropped from the doctoral program in 1931 largely because his philosophy dissertation challenged the notion that education could be advanced by professionalism of this sort. Holmes and Spaulding believed that no dissertation, whatever its field or competence, could be accepted in a true professional school if it challenged the assumptions upon which that school was based.

Holmes sought to extend all aspects of the professional ideal through the thirties with diminishing success. Many kinds of adversity hindered his efforts, and by 1936 the two-year Ed.M. was given up. The search for ways to measure professional success other than by course credits continued, and until the early forties the Ed.M. was awarded on the basis of several lengthy written examinations. But during World War II these efforts too were dropped.

Men argued then, and still argue, that the Depression and the war hardly gave the two-year program a chance; that dwindling income from tuition and endowment forced retrenchments that doomed it. Far from being able to discourage part-timers, Holmes had to urge his faculty in the late thirties to offer courses that would attract as many local teachers as possible.

But the plan would not have succeeded even in the best of times. President Lowell was unimpressed with a conception of professionalism that stressed reforms in institutional procedure above developing a curriculum based on general principles, and rejected outright Holmes' plea for the Harvard Corporation's support in obtaining new buildings. Lowell contended that the School was trying to build a superstructure before it had laid the foundations; that is, it wanted elaborate facilities before it had developed an effective curriculum.

It was true that Holmes, more than Spaulding, had hoped that scholars in the academic disciplines might be appointed to some major positions in the School. In 1930 Truman L. Kelley was appointed to meet Lowell's desire for a statistician, and four years later Holmes brought Robert Ulich from Germany to teach philosophy, history, and comparative education. But these were isolated appointments that were part of no pattern. Kelley had few students, and from the first felt cut off from the main business of the School, which continued to be specific training for specific jobs. The vocationalism that in the twenties had been innovative and exciting became in many instances during the thirties sterile and routine. Holmes criticized Professor John M. Brewer, for example, for using his courses and writing to advocate instead of to analyze vocational guidance long after the pioneer period when advocacy was essential had passed.

From one point of view, that was part of the trouble with the professional ideal. It had not sought to re-examine the ends for which the School existed, but instead had sought to upgrade its product to conform to Harvard tradition. And, less apparent to outsiders than the many procedural changes, the conception of what was appropriate to teach in a school of education did not change at all. Professionalism suggested no new appointment policy. The student body, in addition, changed but little. The School did encourage young college seniors to apply, but few did. Admission depended mainly on collegiate origins: students from "approved" colleges were accepted without question. This admission policy conformed to that of the Faculty of Arts and Sciences, but in the early thirties that faculty upgraded its standards, and could thereafter accuse the School of Education of low standards.

CRISIS AND RE-EXAMINATION

When James Bryant Conant assumed the presidency of Harvard in 1933, the reputation of the School within the University was poor and its finances were precarious. Its separation from the traditional purposes of the University had never been wider. Lowell, unlike Eliot forty years before, had seen no role that the School could play to advance the fortunes of the University or the country. And the School had neglected to search for the general principles that Lowell believed explained the success of other Harvard professional schools.

Conant, on the other hand, thought that the School might still advance the University's purposes by strengthening Harvard's relations with the public schools at a time of sharp class conciousness. Thus Conant tried to bring the School and University closer together by creating the Master of Arts in Teaching program in 1936 and by gaining Corporation support for fund-raising drives in 1937 and 1939. Neither the M.A.T. program nor the fund campaigns met with success. The financial surplus run up during the prosperity of the early twenties began to run out. Tuition and endowment income continued to drop, particularly following the Roosevelt Recession. Serious thoughts were given to dismantling the School if money could not be found to enable it to break even.

The Second World War cut enrollment still further, but also cut expenses as many faculty members entered war work. Near the end of the war, when virtually all the procedures and spirit of the professional ideal had faded, Holmes wrote to a colleague in despair:

Here we are, back nearly to the position we occupied during 1920 to 1927, yet without faculty or staff to do a good job, with quarters crowded and growing shabbier every year, and with no basic principles of operation which will make our program any better than that of any other important university department in our area. In equipment, instruction, contacts with professional groups and the lay public, relations with other departments of the University, research, publication, and the efficient discharge of our routine obligations to students—in everything a Harvard Graduate School has to do—we can claim distinction only in spots and by individual effort. As a School we have little or nothing to be proud of. We are not even working toward goals we have clearly defined. The one instructional distinction we can point to is that we are operating on the graduate level and admitting only qualified students—and that might almost be taken for granted.

In this atmosphere of discouragement, a new opportunity to reconsider the purposes and procedures of the School was unexpectedly provided. Francis T. Spaulding, who had succeeded

Holmes as dean in 1940 but had served only a year and a half before departing for war work, suddenly resigned in late 1945 to become Commissioner of Education of New York. President Conant told the faculty that the financial condition of the School was such that he could not urge Spaulding to stay. Conant then asked Acting Dean Phillip J. Rulon to prepare a memorandum for the Corporation on the School's needs and opportunities. From December until March 1946, members of the faculty worked on the crucial memorandum, the first official effort to recast the purposes of the School since "the professional ideal" had been set forth between 1924 and 1931.

The ideas in the memorandum were not, of course, developed from scratch in a few weeks. Like many such documents, they articulated and codified general trends already in evidence. In the first instance, the composition of the faculty had changed suddenly at the end of the war. Many senior members of the faculty who had embodied the professional ideal had retired or left for other positions. Power in the faculty resided in a group of younger men whose training made them more loyal to academic disciplines than to public-school fields of work. These men were quite conscious that scholarly research had not been an important function of the School before, and they were aware of the wide separation between the Faculty of Education and the Faculty of Arts and Sciences that the professional ideal had promoted and, to some extent, had taken pride in. A few efforts had been made by Spaulding just before the war to initiate productive cross-faculty contacts in public administration and social psychology, but these had not taken hold.

When these men thought about what a school of education should do, they inevitably considered the task of a scholar in such a school. Their solution was to reorient the School toward the study of educational problems rather than to the development of the profession of education. The most important individual in working out this change was Phillip Rulon. Trained at Minnesota in psychology and statistics, he had come to the

School in 1930 with Truman Kelley, and had been responsible for several of the research projects completed in the thirties. He served as acting dean from 1943 until 1948, and wrote a series of reports and memorandums suggesting that the School study the basic problems of educating each generation.

At first Holmes, then a professor one year from retirement, opposed the suggestion that the School's work be arranged according to problems in education rather than jobs. He argued that, if the School were to remain a professional school at all, it had to be strictly vocational: the "pattern of our work as a Faculty (and hence the pattern of our appointments) is set by the way the profession we serve is organized. It is set by the history of education as a profession, not by a theoretical analysis of education as a process occurring in the life of an individual." But Holmes later changed his mind, and asserted that neither he nor Spaulding had conceived of the large possibilities for long-term effects on education through research that Rulon and other members of the faculty had foreseen.

THE RESEARCH IDEAL

The "Purple Memorandum" of March 1946 (so called because of the purple ink used to reproduce it) advocated a school that would look outward toward the solution of educational problems rather than inward toward the professionalizing of education. Like Eliot, like the businessmen who helped form policy just before the First World War, and like Holmes and Spaulding in the late twenties, it saw the uniqueness of the School in its contributions toward changing school practice. But it did not see the School affecting education through quasi-political activity, or through the promotion of social and organizational reform, or through the establishment of a unique professional ideal, but through the work of scholars solving problems through research, and primarily research in the newer social sciences.

The faculty would number about 15, as compared with the 44 that Holmes and Spaulding had thought would be necessary to carry out "the professional ideal." The student body would consist of the equivalent of 100 full-timers, as against the 500 students that Holmes and Spaulding had once anticipated. These students would not be "raw A.B.'s" fresh from college. Rather they would be experienced teachers preparing for positions of leadership in education. No special attention was given to doctoral programs, and there was no expectation that the students would become researchers in the same sense as the faculty. The students would be there, first of all, as an aid and stimulus to the faculty; and second, because the best training for positions of leadership in education was thought to be the exposure to general problems in education through scholars who were trying to solve them.

Thus the Purple Memorandum frankly rejected the conception of the School as making the training sequence identical in pattern to that of other Harvard professional schools; but it stressed general principles in its training programs far more than the School had done in the thirties, and by so doing came far closer to Lowell's conception of proper professional study. Unlike the earlier pattern, the School would not train teachers at all. That task, now seen as rather unimportant, would be continued by the M.A.T. program, if indeed the University wished to continue to train teachers at all.

This new and quite radical conception of the purposes of the School brought it back into connection with the University in two general ways. First, the emphasis on research and the social sciences fitted in not only with the interests of many members of other faculties, thereby promoting professional ties, but also with other developments at Harvard in the integration of social-science disciplines.

Only a few weeks before the Purple Memorandum was finished, the Department of Social Relations was created in the Faculty of Arts and Sciences. President Conant was optimistic about the possibility of producing really useful knowledge in the social sciences, and saw the School of Education as an important part of that effort. In addition, the orientation of the School toward the problems of public education fitted in well with Conant's ideas of the function of a great private university in a democracy. Conant supported the memorandum, and the Corporation approved it as the master plan for the future of the School.

THE SEARCH FOR IDENTITY

It is too early to attempt more than a sketchy review of the growing prosperity of the School that followed the appointment of Francis Keppel as dean in 1948. Keppel clearly intended to carry out the mandate of the Purple Memorandum, and immediately began to build an appropriate faculty. In his first year the faculty was almost doubled in size. The new appointees were typically interested in attacking educational problems from the perspective of the social sciences rather than from that of school experience. Their presence recast the meaning of graduate study in education at Harvard. Where the curriculum had previously been dominated by courses in fields of public-school service, it now became dominated by general courses dealing broadly, often indirectly, with practical educational problems. Keppel later defined the study of education as the "fundamental consideration of man's development and of the structure of society."

Faith in the ability of the social sciences to solve educational problems was great in the late forties and early fifties. A radical revision of the master of education program in 1949-50 virtually eliminated courses in professional specialization in favor of general courses in the social sciences and humanities. But Keppel himself later admitted that the move toward social science had perhaps been excessive and overoptimistic. In 1954 a new series of Ed.M. programs, stressing both general training and preparation for particular careers, was established. And important appointments were made outside the social sciences—in the humanities and in other areas associated with professional specialization in education.

Despite the general adherence to the appointment policy of the Purple Memorandum, the Graduate School of Education became very different from what had been envisioned for it in 1946. Neither the faculty nor the student body remained small, and research did not become the School's most important contribution. The character of the Keppel regime, and the special problems it and its successor had to face, can best be understood in terms of how the School deviated from the course it had been expected to take.

The Purple Memorandum was framed in an atmosphere of gloom and crisis. The large professional school envisioned in the thirties by Holmes and Spaulding seemed impossible to achieve, even pretentious and undesirable. Past experience suggested that the School could not have both size and quality. Hence a small student body was called for. A small faculty was also thought necessary, since a large one appeared financially unthinkable and extremely difficult to recruit. President Conant praised the Purple Memorandum not simply because it echoed his own confidence that social science could solve educational problems; its financial realism also appealed to him. The School of Education had learned from its troubled past.

Keppel and his associates, however, operated in a different financial climate from that of 1946. Immediately after becoming dean, he received considerable financial support from both the Carnegie Corporation and the Harvard governing boards. In subsequent years the Rockefeller, Kellogg, and Ford foundations, among others, supplied large sums for the initiation of new projects. Additional funds, often to increase the School's endowment, came from members of the Overseers' Visiting Committee. Finally, in the late fifties the federal government began to contribute increasingly larger sums for research, development, and financial aid to students. The emergence of these three ources of financing was sudden and unexpected. They allowed the School to become more ambitious than anyone had foreseen in 1946. But the kind of support they provided was usually temporary rather than permanent. There was no assurance that the expanded activities of the School would continue if the temporary support from external sources was withdrawn.

The most striking deviation from the 1946 plan was Keppel's emphasis on teacher education and the M.A.T. program. The Purple Memorandum had dismissed teacher education, but Keppel made it the central business of the School. Not only was money poured into the M.A.T. program; in 1951 a parallel program was established to train teachers for elementary schools. No action could have been more contrary to the spirit of the Purple Memorandum, or more characteristic of the Keppel regime.

It is easy to point to numerous external factors to account for Keppel's interest in the education of teachers: a severe national teacher shortage in the 1950's; public criticism of traditional methods of teacher education, which gave new prestige to the M.A.T. idea; the availability of foundation money to support this activity rather than others.

At Harvard many of the old antagonists had retired or had lost interest in the battles of the thirties. Genuine cooperation between the Faculties of Arts and Sciences and Education, or at least benign apathy, made a stable and reasonable program possible for the first time.

But the School's continuing interest in teacher education is not understandable in terms of these events alone. Keppel was not merely responding to "national needs" or to the possibility of obtaining money. He had a general plan, which later became a well-articulated strategy for improving public education in America: to raise the quality of men and women who chose careers in the schools. The Graduate School of Education had to attract young graduates of the best colleges, just those people who rarely entered public education.

On the face of it, there was nothing novel in this desire.

Holmes' two-year Ed.M. had been specifically designed fo
young graduates of liberal arts colleges. Holmes had spent hi
energies, however, on establishing an elaborate pattern of train
ing based on the pattern already worked out at other Harvar
professional schools. He had been more concerned with th
nature of the training program than with getting first-rate stu
dents to enter it. Of course Holmes thought about the problem
of attracting liberal arts graduates: when the two-year progra
was established he attempted to send descriptive literature t
30,000 college seniors! But he always thought the best advertise
ment was large, prosperous, visible activity in Cambridge. Onc
again, the other Harvard professional schools, and particularl
the handsome new Business School and its campus, provided
model.

In the fifties the Graduate School of Education became les
interested in the nature and content of its teacher-training pro
grams than in the quality of students who were attracted t
them. Several novel recruiting plans were developed: the 195
cooperative plan, whereby prestigious liberal arts college
joined with Harvard to encourage more of their graduates t
consider careers in teaching; the establishment of a separate of
fice for recruiting in 1959; and the creation of lucrative priz
fellowships in the 1960's. From 1948 to 1960 the amount of fi
nancial aid dispensed annually by the School rose from $41,60
to $850,000. The School did attract students from first-rate col
leges, and could point to test scores and other data to show thei
increasing quality. The content of the training programs, how
ever, changed but little: the director of the M.A.T. program sai
in 1962 that Harvard's curriculum and pedagogy in teacher train
ing was "little altered from that of 1920."

The recruitment problem could not be solved merely by finan
cial aid and talk of challenges. Keppel gradually realized tha
the School's difficulty in attracting large numbers of able student
stemmed in large part from the unattractiveness of educationa
careers themselves. Consequently, he sought ways for the Schoo

of Education to effect changes in educational career patterns. In two remarkable annual reports for 1954-55 and 1955-56, comparable in excitement and originality to Rulon's influential reports, Keppel discussed the problem of educational careers and suggested team teaching as one device for creating new educational jobs of greater power and responsibility.

Most important, he asserted that Harvard should not simply talk about such innovations but should "take part in actual programs of experiment and demonstration in schools." The result was the School and University Program for Research and Development (SUPRAD), a cooperative venture between Harvard and local school systems designed to turn ideas into practices and institutions. The desire to improve education by attracting to it young people of ability thus became not just a "recruiting" enterprise but a research and development enterprise as well. In fact, the search for a first-rate student body touched most activities of the School. A major revision of the doctoral program to train administrators, for example, included not just curriculum changes but elaborate techniques to recruit and assess applicants.

The emphasis on young students in master's degree programs implies no change in appointment policy. The faculty has become increasingly dominated by men trained in the social sciences, humanities, and other scholarly disciplines. Numerous new research units such as the Laboratory of Human Development, the Laboratory for Research in Instruction, the Center for Field Studies, and, more recently, the Center for Research and Development on Educational Differences, celebrate the virtues of teamwork and cooperation with public schools and other Harvard faculties.

One of the most significant characteristics of this research-oriented faculty is its growing interest in systematic training programs to produce young scholars and teachers of the same stamp as itself. The production and perpetuation of scholars through training programs, a central function of important graduate schools of arts and sciences, was a rather new and unexplored idea at the Graduate School of Education in the early fifties. In earlier years, most of the scholars on the faculty trained up very few men to carry on what they had done. But as the fifties progressed a larger number of doctorates were awarded to students who would carry on in research, mainly in fields where organized settings for scholarly apprenticeship had developed at Harvard, such as the Laboratory of Human Development. In the mid-sixties, however, this number has remained small in relation to the total number of students in the School.

The situation has been paradoxical. On the one hand, the appointment policy has produced a large faculty composed mainly of scholars. On the other hand, the School's recruiting strategy has enrolled most students in master's programs, which are largely responsible for its growing national reputation. These programs have prepared students for careers in schools, not careers in research. There has been little deliberate effort to recruit students who would follow the careers of the faculty. Indeed, an anomaly of the Purple Memorandum was its juxtaposition of a research-oriented faculty on a student body of experienced schoolmen.

The faculty Keppel created eventually came to question the training programs he had most relied on. By 1965, "doctoral potential" became an important admission criterion for nearly every program in the School. Even those faculty members most closely identified with teacher training—the men in the various teaching fields—developed doctoral programs in curriculum and instruction. They saw the M.A.T. program not as an end in itself but as a recruiter and feeder for their doctoral programs.

When a faculty committee once again reviewed the purposes of the School in 1965 the atmosphere was strikingly different from that of 1946. No atmosphere of crisis prevailed. The School was more prosperous financially, though it still lacked the permanent resources necessary to accomplish all that it wished. Radical changes in the content of instruction seemed improbable: unlike the situation in the immediate postwar period, the pernanent faculty was young and growing. It was no longer possible to create immediately an entire faculty according to some master plan.

Reassessment had to proceed along different lines. First, the faculty could turn inward, as it had not done systematically since the late twenties, to examine the organization, length, and timing of its instruction. Second, it could try to resolve the growing problem of what kind of student body might best benefit from the faculty's interests and character. These questions touch programs and students more than faculty appointment policy, but their answers, no less than the decisions of 1946, might alter once again the shape of the School.

APPENDIX B

FACULTY ACTION ON THE REPORT

The faculty of the Graduate School of Education began to discuss the report of the Committee on the Graduate Study of Education late in 1964–65. Debate continued in monthly faculty meetings in 1965–66, ending in March 1966. The following elements of the report were endorsed by the faculty.

The first recommendations adopted dealt with the faculty's own organization. The suggested creation of six faculty "areas" recognized the need of a growing faculty both for decentralization and for structure in curriculum and policy formation. Three of the areas formed are "clinical"—administration, guidance, and teaching—and three are "disciplinary"—humanities, psychology, and social sciences.

Further, a permanent Committee on Academic Policy, to guide the School's academic affairs more systematically, was established. The function of overseeing students' degree work, formerly the province of several committees, was given to a new Committee on Degrees. Similar functional economies were made by creating the Committee on Research and Development and the Committee on Admissions, which also handles recruitment of students, financial aid, and placement. The major business of the faculty is thus carried on by four standing committees.

Most significantly, the faculty adopted the recommendation to shift a greater portion of its resources to doctoral study. At the same time, it committed itself to strengthening the "clinical" master's degree programs in roughly the form the committee had recommended. (The year of internship was not mandated as necessarily coming during the second year; it could come first.)

The faculty voted to eliminate a master's degree obtained through summer study only.

The master's degree in certain fields—human development, measurement and statistics, and research in instruction—was retained, to be developed along clinical lines, including also a suitable internship in the second year. The Master of Education for General Purposes was retained as an exploratory one-year program for a very small number of able students for whom no other degree seems appropriate. This latter vote was contrary to the recommendation of the report.

The faculty voted to expand postdoctoral study and to conduct special academic-year and summer short-term institutes on a variety of special topics to meet more immediate and pressing professional and instructional needs.

A doctoral colloquium, proposed as a device for better integrating the several areas of the School for the student, has been planned. The colloquium is to be conducted on a trial basis for one year under the direction of a student board.

Continued detailed consideration of the report will continue during the 1966–67 academic year.

APPENDIX C

SOME EXAMPLES OF DOCTORAL STUDY

There are two kinds of doctoral degrees in education offered at Harvard. One is the Doctor of Education degree, which is governed by the Faculty of Education alone. The other is the Ph.D. in Education, which is offered under the Faculty of Arts and Sciences and is governed jointly by that faculty and by the Faculty of Education. For both degrees, students pursue a rigorous course of interdisciplinary study and independent research that culminates in the writing of a dissertation or, in some instances of the Ed.D., a report on a project.

DOCTOR OF EDUCATION

The purpose and design of the Ed.D. vary. One pattern, for example, is "clinical"; the so-called "clinical areas"—administration, guidance, and teaching—view the Ed.D. as a professional degree that gives evidence of the holder's competence to deal with actual situations in a given area. The degree gains its legitimacy primarily from its relation to the School's concern for solving problems of educational practice, and secondarily from its association with the scholarly disciplines. In addition, the clinical Ed.D. gives evidence not only that the holder can deal with clinical situations but also that he is competent to contribute to further description and better understanding of clinical practice, or perhaps to create more effective practice. This second condition requires that he be seen as more than a master craftsman, whether curriculum designer, teacher, supervisor, or administrator; it requires that he be able to contribute to the growth of understanding the process of teaching, supervision, administration, or guidance.

Degrees in administration and in guidance are offered, along with five doctoral programs in teaching in the clinical areas: English education, mathematics education, the teaching of reading, science education, and social studies education.

The Ed.D. that is "disciplinary," wholly within a scholarly field, is offered in the sociology of education, the history and philosophy of education, human development, research in instruction, and measurement and statistics. A study is under way to determine whether the last three fields can be more suitably offered and grouped under the field of educational psychology. The faculty is also considering doctoral programs in the economics and politics of education within the social sciences area.

Programs leading to the Ed.D. consist of five "stages," each stage usually being equivalent to one year. The general sequence of stages is suggested in the accompanying chart, though much flexibility is possible. In a number of programs, students may enter doctoral study at Stage I without a master's degree or prior experience in education. Many students, however, are admitted to doctoral study at the beginning of Stage III, with the master's degree and at least one year of supervised internship or other relevant experience. The chart, with its general plan, represents only a guide; students with unusual preparation may, for example, be admitted at the beginning of Stage IV.

A candidate's program can be determined only after he has registered, met with his adviser, filed his study plan, and received the approval of the Committee on Degrees. Particular programs may require preparation in foreign languages, mathematics, or statistics, but there are no general requirements that apply to all students.

The minimum residence period, required by University statute, is one year for students entering with the master's degree and two years for students entering with the bachelor's degree. Al-

THE FIVE STAGES OF DOCTORAL STUDY

Stage I	Stage II	Stage III	Stage IV	Stage V
Course work required for master's degree	Clinical internship required for master's degree	Advanced course work required for Ed.D.	Course work, seminars, independent study	Dissertation or project
			Qualifying paper	
			Plan for dissertation or project	

Admission and assignment of adviser (at Stages I, III, or IV)

Evaluation of study plan (at outset of doctoral study; candidate may amend as study proceeds)

Stage IV	Stage V
Final approval of study plan	
Approval of qualifying paper topic	
Submission and evaluation of qualifying paper	
Appointment of *ad hoc* committee	
Submission of dissertation or project plan; evaluation by *ad hoc* committee; and oral examination by *ad hoc* com-	Submission of dissertation or project report; final oral examination on project report by *ad hoc committee*

though candidates rarely finish in the minimum time, they are expected to complete all requirements no later than seven years after they first register.

Normally at the end of Stage III or during Stage IV, the student applies to the Committee on Degrees for permission to write a qualifying paper. This paper, usually no longer than fifty pages, should identify and analyze an educational problem. It represents a test of the candidate's ability to gather and sort data, to analyze relevant literature critically and succinctly, or perhaps to conduct a pilot study that will lead to the dissertation or project. The candidate does not consult members of the faculty during the writing of his paper. After the Committee on Degrees has approved the topic, the student has six months to complete it.

Once the qualifying paper is approved, the student presents his dissertation or project topic in extended written form to a special *ad hoc* committee appointed by the Committee on Degrees that then conducts an oral examination. When the candidate has convinced this committee that his dissertation or project plan is both wise and practicable, he is allowed to proceed. Examples of recent successful qualifying papers are "Commitment: Its Nature and Development in Late Adolescence," "The Structure of Metaphor: A Critical Examination of Recent Descriptions," "Political versus Professional Control of Education," "A Critical Discussion of the Term 'Structure' as It Functions in Recent Educational Theory," "A Pilot Experiment to Reexamine Levin's Hypothesis Concerning a 'Set for Diversity' in Beginning Reading," "The Liberal Journals and American Education, 1914–21," "State Aid to Education in Massachusetts," and "Negro Children's Stories about School as Compared with Stories of Puerto Rican Children."

The dissertation may consist of an experimental investigation, a critical analysis of educational problems, issues, developments or a field of study, or an analytical study of some field of educational practice. Some recent dissertations are "The Measurement of Children's Perception of Difficulty in Reading Materials,"

"Some Relationships among Learning, Practice, and Recall," "The Irony of Urban School Reform: Ideology and Style in Mid-Nineteenth Century Massachusetts," "Voluntary Motor Control and Time Estimates in Relation to Learning Deficit," and "Personality Measures in College Admission."

The project represents an alternative to the dissertation that is available in some programs as the final requirement for the Ed.D. The candidate assumes major responsibility for defining, planning, and carrying out a significant task, usually in a school system. From time to time he presents reports to the faculty members who are observing and evaluating the project. The final report includes a statement justifying the goals of the project and the procedures used, analysis of the crucial incidents that arose, consideration of the accomplishments of the project in relation to its intent, and a critical review of the administration of the project. Several recent projects are "The Establishment of Office of Education Assistance to Urban School System Planning," "The In-Service Training of Elementary School Teachers in Science," and "The Planning, Organization, and Teaching of a Course in the Motion Picture as an Art Form: A Project in Curriculum Development and Implementation."

All programs require full-time study at least through completion of the qualifying paper. However, the Committee on Degrees interprets the requirement flexibly, and teaching fellowships, research assistantships, and similar work may usefully replace the usual full-time requirement of four half courses per semester.

Three examples of "clinical" programs—mathematics education, social studies education, and the Administrative Career Program —and two examples of "disciplinary" programs—human development and the sociology of education—follow.

MATHEMATICS EDUCATION

The doctoral program is designed to prepare the candidate for some or all of the following positions: secondary classroom teaching; elementary teaching, as a mathematics specialist; work as a department head or supervisor in a school system; teaching subject-matter and methods courses, and supervising practice teaching in a college or university teacher-training program; full-time work on curriculum development projects; or work as a curriculum specialist in a state department of education.

Admission to the doctoral program requires at least the level of training and experience associated with the Master of Arts in Teaching degree at Harvard, with superior performance in both academic work and classroom teaching. The program consists of four elements, as follows.

1. Mathematical training in depth, to the extent of a dozen or more half courses taken in the Department of Mathematics under the Faculty of Arts and Sciences, starting at the level of differential and integral calculus. A typical sequence might begin with this course and continue with introductory courses in higher algebra, higher geometry, theory of numbers, mathematical probability, and functions of the real variable, with later courses being selected in accordance with the interests and intentions of the candidate.

2. Special courses in mathematics and its relation to teaching offered by the Faculty of Education, which include elementary mathematics from an advanced standpoint and a doctoral seminar.

3. Course work in measurement and in the history, philosophy, and sociology of education, at or above the general level required for the M.A.T.

4. Electives chosen to suit the program of the individual student, which might well include extended study of cognitive psychology, especially for those specializing in elementary education. For such candidates, psychology courses could replace some of the advanced mathematics courses that would otherwise be taken.

The requirements described above are intended only as descriptions of levels of achievement. Ordinarily some of them would be satisfied by work done before admission to doctoral candidacy.

The work represented by the qualifying paper and dissertation may range over a broad spectrum, from practical expertise at one end to creative contributions to teaching at the other. Work toward the dissertation nearly always includes a practicum in teaching or supervision, or both. The candidate's program usually includes experience in both, with the aid of course work as needed.

Thus some dissertations are, in effect, project reports of practical undertakings such as improving the mathematics curriculum and staff of a school by working in the school as a classroom teacher, in-service training director, or resident supervisor of student teachers. In such cases, the qualifying paper is a forecast of the work that the dissertation will report and analyze.

At the other end of the spectrum are dissertations based on the development of original teaching materials by the candidate. In these cases it is expected that the materials will have been tried out and that the results will be reported in the dissertation. When the new materials are substantially original, however, they may be regarded as the main substance of the dissertation, and its acceptance will be predicted essentially on a favorable judgment of their quality.

In any case, it is expected that the clinical dissertation will include a thoughtful, analytical account of what has happened, but it will be regarded as a case study rather than as a scientific demonstration of a hypothesis.

SOCIAL STUDIES EDUCATION

The purpose of the doctoral program is to prepare students to design, implement, or evaluate new programs and practices in the teaching of social studies in the schools, or a combination of these. The programs and practices generally cut across four fields: curriculum; teaching, including self-instruction; supervision; and diagnosis and assessment of students' attitudes, concepts, language, and strategies of argumentation.

In all these fields a number of decisions must be made, either consciously or implicitly, before design, development, or implementation of new practices can be carried out. These decisions involve selecting materials of instruction; determining the scope and sequence of what is to be covered by the materials, how they are to be presented, types of media to be used, motivation devices, and so forth; and predicting what may occur between student and teacher, student and student, or teacher and supervisor.

Behind these decisions lie three types of problems. First is the extent to which the learning outcomes that rationalize a program or practice are grounded in a realistic view of society and are consistent with a justifiable statement of the ethical and epistemological grounding of that view; second, the extent to which specific pedagogical decisions are grounded in or clarified by some systematic approach to learning; and third, the extent to which programs or practices make assumptions about the nature and stability of present institutional arrangements within which change is to take place. The doctoral program trains the candidate to examine critically these types of instructional decisions, to test their adequacy against standards of knowledge evolved in the program, and to make a creative contribution, not only to the practice of teaching social studies, but also to the establishment of new standards.

A schematic summary of the doctoral program in social studies education follows.

First year. The first year is preceded by teaching apprenticeship during the summer. During the academic year, the student takes a course in political or social theory, a general course in the behavioral sciences, two electives in history or social science under the Faculty of Arts and Sciences, and, in the Graduate School of Education, the course entitled American School: Introduction to Education, and a curriculum and methods course in secondary school social studies.

Second year. Teaching internship.

Third year. In addition to a year-long proseminar in social studies education, the student elects a course in philosophy, history, or social science; a course in the meaning of explanation in history and the social sciences; courses in the technology of quantitative research in education, including statistics and introduction to computer techniques; and courses related to his field of specialization.

Fourth year. In the third summer and/or the fourth year of the program, the candidate is hired as a paid doctoral apprentice in supervision or curriculum, or both. The work in supervision may be done either in the Harvard-Newton summer school or during the regular academic year. The apprenticeship in curriculum development is usually carried on within the framework of an existing program, such as the Harvard Social Studies Project or at Educational Services Incorporated. This work might involve the writing or editing of teaching materials; preparing units of instruction; developing tests; experimental teaching; coding and statistical work; problems of research design; or working with teachers in a school to promote acceptance of a new program. In addition to the apprenticeship, the student takes further courses in his field of specialization and prepares his qualifying paper and then a prospectus for doctoral internship, concluding with an oral examination.

Fifth year. This year is designated as a doctoral internship and is devoted exclusively to the design, development, and research interests of the candidate. Admission to doctoral internship assumes that the candidate has written a successful qualifying paper in his special field and that he has presented and been examined on a research plan for the internship. The internship is followed by submission of the dissertation.

ADMINISTRATIVE CAREER PROGRAM

Study in administration at Harvard combines graduate work in the social sciences with the case approach, and requires two years' residence beyond a relevant master's degree. In this program, administration as a narrow technical task of executing the precise commands of superior authorities is rejected in favor of viewing the school administrator as being always a judge of values and frequently a determiner of policies. It is argued that the administrator therefore needs education in the study of values: his own, those of the community, those of the persons with whom he must defend his policies, and those argued and transmitted from history. He needs, furthermore, an education going beyond the techniques of carrying out the orders of others into the procedures by which he may capably assist the makers of public policy.

First year. In the first resident year beyond the master's degree, students take courses under the Faculty of Education in elements of educational administration, problems of curriculum development, social organization of schools and the community, financial support and business management of education, and, under the Faculty of Arts and Sciences, a course in urban policy problems. During the first semester, in connection with this last course, each student spends one day a week in a local community and is placed with an administrative officer who has central responsibilities in a local government. In the latter part of the semester the student works with an administrator in a school system. In addition, the student takes two electives.

Second year. The core of this year is a field study of a community and its schools in which faculty and graduate students work together. Recent studies have been undertaken in communities facing problems of *de facto* segregation: Hartford, Connecticut; Englewood, New Jersey; Wilmington, Delaware; and Pittsburgh, Pennsylvania. In addition to the field study, the student takes courses in advanced cases and concepts in educational administration, theory and practice in educational administration, and three electives.

Following the formal period of study, the student takes an appropriate job in a school or other educational institution, normally away from Cambridge, and completes his program by carrying out there an administrative project that leads to a final project report.

Examples of doctoral programs in the "disciplinary" areas are those in human development and in the sociology of education.

HUMAN DEVELOPMENT

The purpose of the program is to develop and explore psychological concepts of value to educational practitioners and to prepare students for college teaching and research on those aspects of the behavioral sciences that are of greatest actual value or potential use in the understanding of the educational process. Practical experiences are varied in order to familiarize the student with as complete a range of child growth and development as possible. Settings for such field experiences include public and private schools from nursery through college levels; day care centers; special community educational programs; remedial reading centers; speech and hearing agencies; outpatient and residential institutions for treatment of emotionally disturbed, retarded, deaf, blind, aphasic, and other atypical children; and pediatric clinics. Whenever possible, field training is provided in cross-cultural settings. An effort is made to integrate the content of course work in human development with experiences in these educational settings in order to help the student identify major research needs and opportunities in these areas.

A key feature of the program is the emphasis on both formal and informal apprenticeship in research, starting in the student's first graduate year. Apprenticeship is broadly defined as including not only a close working relationship with a faculty member who is himself engaged in research but also exposure to the general atmosphere of productive investigatory work. Research activities include studies of individual and cultural differences in the development of cognitive abilities, personality and attitude changes, motivation and self-concept, and social grouping.

Course patterns for the doctorate in human development are flexible, and an individual program is prescribed in consultation with each student. Courses are usually selected in the Departments of Social Relations, Psychology, Government, Statistics, and Linguistics of the Faculty of Arts and Sciences and in the Graduate School of Education. Course work is carefully integrated with the practicum. As indicated above, research apprenticeships are provided throughout the student's training.

The following program outlines one suggested pattern of courses in human development.

First year. The student takes a course in development of personality and social behavior, courses in educational research and statistics, and two electives. A part-time research apprenticeship is sometimes arranged.

Second year. The student takes a course either in human development as related to schools and schooling in a cross-cultural perspective or in the sociology of school systems; and courses in research methods in child study and in problems of curriculum development. In addition, he takes two electives and engages in research apprenticeship.

Third and fourth years. The student continues his individual plan of courses and research apprenticeship; completes the qualifying paper and oral examination; and completes his dissertation.

SOCIOLOGY OF EDUCATION

Students in this program are systematically exposed to substantive problems of the general field of sociology and of the sociology of education. They are required to take courses and seminars in research methods and to engage in a set of related experiences that provide them with the skills required to conduct competent research. The program attempts to make maximum use of the resources of the Department of Social Relations and other centers and departments in the University as well as those of the Graduate School of Education.

First year. The first year places heavy emphasis on the student's introduction to key perspectives and concepts of sociology, its major theoretical ideas, the types of problems sociologists investigate, and bodies of empirical findings in selected problem areas. Four of the eight courses each student takes are ordinarily selected from among those offered by the Department of Social Relations, under the Faculty of Arts and Sciences, in the social structure of the United States, the study of small groups, social stratification, urban sociology, an approach to a general theory of action, and a proseminar. The student also begins his study of statistcal methods and research design. He is expected to take two courses in the following group: statistics in the social sciences, quantitative methods in social research, educational statistics, the computer in education, data processing in educational research, or survey methods in education and social research.

The remainder of course work during the first year is devoted to a full-year proseminar on the sociology of education. The first half of the proseminar focuses on the historical development of the sociology of education and provides an overview of past and current research in the field. Several sessions are devoted to presentations by sociologists of education at other universities who discuss their own research. The student is required to read intensively in the literature and to examine critically a set of major works in the field. The second part of the proseminar is designed to require the student to cope with the problems of raising significant questions for sociological examination, developing hypotheses that can be systematically examined and obtaining data to test them.

Second year. This year stresses intensive work in the study of sociology as it is related to problems of education. All students are required to take a year-long seminar in research in the sociology of education. This seminar is designed to allow students to participate in the several major phases of research inquiry, including the design of a study, development of a hypothesis, construction of instruments, field work activities, data analysis, and reporting of research findings. The seminar is based on an ongoing research study or one especially developed for instructional purposes.

The student selects three additional courses or seminars in the sociology of education, in accordance with his special interest, in the Graduate School of Education or in the Department of Social Relations. These might include courses in the social organization of the school and community, comparative organizational analysis, analysis of educational roles, research issues in the sociology of higher education, anatomy and control of complex organizations, comparative child rearing, public opinion and mass communication, behavior problems in childhood and adolescence, research problems in urban sociology, research methods in the study of small groups, and group conflict and prejudices.

The remaining courses of the second year are divided between those in educational and research methodology, depending on the student's special area of interest, his qualifying paper and oral examination, and planning his dissertation.

Third year. The major activity during this year is research for the dissertation. Some students carry out independent studies, and others work on aspects of problems under study by members of the faculty or in various research centers of the University.

PH.D. IN EDUCATION

The Ph.D. in Education is offered under the Faculty of Arts and Sciences but is governed by a committee composed of members of that faculty and of the Faculty of Education. The candidate has two advisers, one from each of the two faculties. There is a language requirement, which varies according to the department in which the student is enrolled, and there are general examinations sometime during Stage III (see chart above), rather than the qualifying paper that is required for the Ed.D. The general examinations have two parts: the examination in special fields, and the general orals.

Each candidate must demonstrate competence in two special fields he has chosen, usually by two three-hour written examinations, one set by the adviser in the Faculty of Arts and Sciences, the other by the adviser in the Faculty of Education. The advisers may exercise considerable latitude in the examination procedure. Oral examinations and special papers of publishable quality are sometimes substituted for or combined with written examinations. A single written examination set by the two advisers together is also sometimes used. Once the candidate has satisfied his advisers in one of these ways that he has an adequate mastery of his special fields, the advisers ask the chairman of the committee to set a general oral examination by the committee as a whole. The intent of this examination is to test the candidate's ability to apply his special knowledge to the general field of education.

The dissertation is intended to be an original contribution to knowledge in the student's special field.

APPENDIX D

STATISTICS

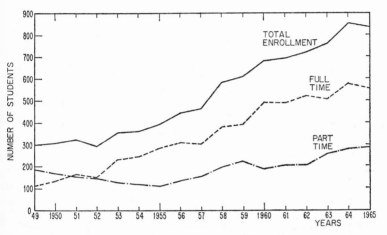

CHART 1. Enrollment in the Harvard Graduate School of Education, 1949–1965 (spring catalogue figures).

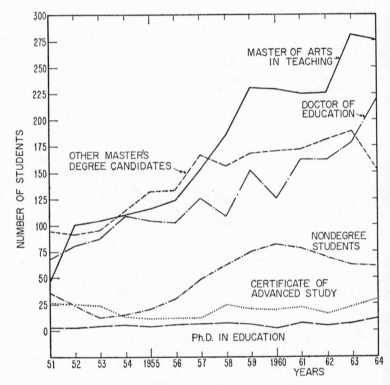

CHART 2. Enrollment in programs of the Harvard Graduate School of Education, 1951–1964 (fall registration figures). Nondegree students include John Hay Fellows and those enrolled in the Academic Year Institute.

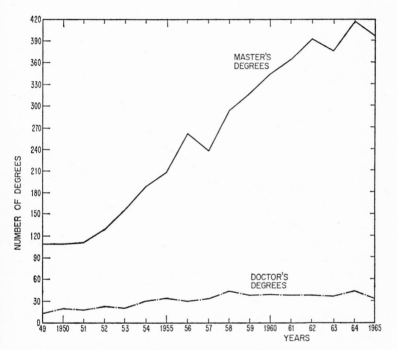

CHART 3. Degrees awarded by the Harvard Graduate School of Education, 1949–1965.

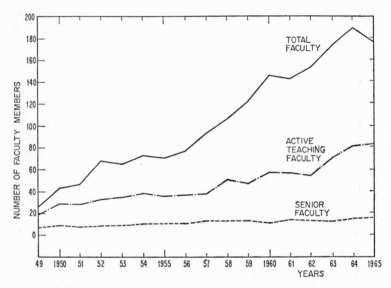

CHART 4. Faculty of the Harvard Graduate School of Education, 1949–1965. Total faculty = all personnel listed as "Faculty" in catalogue (including research associates, teaching fellows, administrators, etc.); active teaching faculty = dean, professors, associate professors, lecturers, assistant professors, instructors; senior faculty = dean, professors, associate professors.

Harvard Graduate School of Education,
actual expenditures, 1955–1965

Year	Endowment principal	Total income	Total expenses	Government funds included in total expenses
1954–55	$3,263,735	$718,321	$819,691	$8,552
1955–56	3,467,896	718,626	789,774	38,710
1956–57	4,147,977	902,801	909,374	329,617
1957–58	4,455,039	1,188,805	1,192,243	322,249
1958–59	4,801,164	1,689,905	1,675,120	374,660
1959–60	5,599,963	2,095,310	2,096,533	482,567
1960–61	5,825,027	2,482,292	2,490,271	648,803
1961–62	6,255,146	2,976,416	2,970,946	755,314
1962–63	6,358,525	3,325,069	3,334,059	769,595
1963–64	8,784,018	3,499,608	3,463,992	1,042,560
1964–65	10,603,431	4,340,865	4,236,075	1,868,840

INDEX